A Multicultural/Multimodal/Multisystems Approach to Working with Culturally Different Families

SHARON-ANN GOPAUL-MCNICOL

Westport, Connecticut
London

Library of Congress Cataloging-in-Publication Data

Gopaul-McNicol, Sharon-ann.
    A multicultural/multimodal/multisystems approach to working with
culturally different families / Sharon-ann Gopaul-McNicol.
        p.   cm.
    Includes bibliographical references and index.
    ISBN 0–275–95560–5 (alk. paper)
    1. Cultural psychiatry. 2. Psychiatry, Transcultural. I. Title.
RC455.4.E8G67 1997
    616.89—DC20   96–33195

British Library Cataloguing in Publication Data is available.

Library of Congress Catalog Card Number: 96–33195
ISBN: 0–275–95560–5

First published in 1997

Praeger Publishers, 88 Post Road West, Westport, CT 06881
An imprint of Greenwood Publishing Group, Inc.

Printed in the United States of America

The paper used in this book complies with the
Permanent Paper Standard issued by the National
Information Standards Organization (Z39.48–1984).

10 9 8 7 6 5 4 3 2 1

To Ulric and Monique Mandisa
With love, gratitude, tenderness, and respect
and in loving memory of my father, St. Elmo Gopaul

Contents

Preface

This book is the culmination of ten years of cross-cultural practice, research, consultation, and supervision with families of various ethnic and cultural backgrounds. As I developed, implemented, and served as a consultant to various educational and clinical institutions throughout the United States and the Caribbean, I came to realize that a different approach to psychotherapy and tutelage is needed if culturally different families are to smoothly acculturate in this society.

My work led me to conclude that a new model, a more comprehensive approach to intervention, is needed to best address the needs of these diverse populations. The Multicultural/Multimodal/Multisystems (MULTI-CMS) approach was developed after assessing over 2,400 children in the school setting and working with 873 individuals in a clinical capacity.

This book introduces a model for intellectual assessment—a bio-ecological approach—and a model for psychotherapy—the MULTI-CMS approach. The principal objective of these models is to help mental health professionals more accurately assess and treat individuals from various ethnic, cultural, and linguistic backgrounds. The techniques and strategies proposed by these models are indicative of an eclecticism, ranging from cognitive behavioral interventions to multimodes and multisystems approaches to treatment. From a humanistic perspective these models allow for unconditional positive regard, that is, acceptance of individuals who are different. The MULTI-CMS approach allows the therapist to view the world through the lenses of the client. Finally, from an ethnocultural/ethnopsychological perspective, this model has endorsed the assumption that each cultural set of circumstances results in a unique response and coping style, crucial to one's personality development.

The theoretical bases for the MULTI-CMS model originated from research done in cross-cultural psychology and cross-cultural mental health with ethnic minorities in the United States and people who come from colonized systems around the world. As such, this model has three categories where change can be effected: individual, institutional, and societal. In other words, this model seeks to empower the client through interactions with these various systems. Moreover, individual and societal goals focus on the elimination of the impediments to the development of a true multicultural society in which each person's individuality is respected. Therefore with this model, the diversity of the client is viewed as a catalyst to the development of the therapist.

In summary, the MULTI-CMS model produces a useful set of tools, a worldview that allows everyone to live in a pluralistic society without being seen as inferior, but rather as different in a positive way.

OVERVIEW

This book is divided into four parts. Part I examines historical and contemporary perspectives of the influence of culture on an individual's functioning (Chapter 1). This section also gives a wake-up call to the mental health field with respect to the need for an ethical mandate to examine alternatives to traditional assessment and counseling techniques (Chapter 2).

Part II explores intellectual assessment issues (Chapter 3) with the culturally different. Chapter 4 focuses on educational and visual motor assessment and its applicability with culturally diverse clients. Chapter 5 highlights ways of misassessing and misdiagnosing the personality of culturally different individuals. Best practices in report writing for the linguistically and culturally different client are examined in Chapter 6.

Part III offers treatment interventions with a focus on salient issues to be cognizant of (Chapter 7) when counseling the culturally different. Chapter 8 examines the major treatment approaches in counseling the culturally different, while the MULTI-CMS model for treatment is explored in detail in Chapter 9. Two case studies of linguistically and culturally diverse families are presented in Chapter 10.

Part IV offers training suggestions for mental health workers with an emphasis on the major competencies needed for developing one's multicultural skills (Chapter 11). Finally, a vision for the mental health field for the future is proposed via a multisystem interdisciplinary approach (Chapter 12).

Acknowledgments

While I recognize that an author tends to use the acknowledgment section to thank his or her professional colleagues, for this book I want to utilize this opportunity to thank solely the four people who have most profoundly influenced my personal and professional life. In my future projects which are all co-authored publications, I will express my gratitude to the many professional colleagues and personal friends who have been instrumental in my overall development. Since I may not have the opportunity for quite awhile to singly author another book, I must say to my darling husband of eighteen years, my precious daughter, and my wonderful parents, thank you.

I could not have asked for a more beautiful family. I am grateful every day for you, and I hope that in a small way, I have brought to you half of the joy that you have brought to me.

PART I

Historical and Contemporary Perspectives on the Influence of Culture in Psychology and Other Mental Health Areas

1
Historical Perspectives on Multiculturalism

Historically, in the United States, the worldview of the culturally different client is linked to the experiences of oppression and racism. This is because counseling, in and of itself, does not take place in a vacuum independent of the sociopolitical influences of the larger society. Culture represents the values, customs, beliefs, heritage, and norms of a particular group of people from a particular society. Thus, the cultural process allows for the transmission of certain social values from one generation to another. As such, psychology, since its origin, has always been strongly influenced by culture.

Multiculturalism has a long-established history which is not unique to the American culture. People from around the world have always recognized the difficulty of communicating with people from different cultural backgrounds. An examination of history suggests that this situation will continue to exist as long as people are racially, culturally, religiously, and politically different. The difficulty has come not only because we are different, but also because the traditions, values, and beliefs of people different from the dominant majority are not often respected and recognized. History has shown that the ease with which immigrants have assimilated in the United States depends upon their race and cultural similarity to the dominant group (Gushue & Sciarra, 1995).

In the 1950s and 1960s many minority authors echoed the feelings of their clients with respect to their views on counseling—that White counselors "do not accept, respect and understand cultural differences" (Pine, 1972, p. 35). This is because mental health professionals, as any others in society, are products of the social trainings of their cultures. They too define the "normal" family as the middle-upper-class White American family and compared their clients against that norm. Thus the implicit assumptions in the theories of mental health workers were oftentimes never examined in the context of the culturally different client. Thus the difficulties in intercultural relationships were often seen as problems stemming from the client in accepting treatment, rather than from issues of cultural differences.

Around the early 1970s the terms *cross-cultural counseling* and *multicultural counseling* had begun to emerge in the psychology literature, since the counseling profession had come to recognize that the techniques and interventions being implemented were inadequate for working with culturally different people. It was around this time that a more pluralistic perspective in counseling emerged and scholars began to question the validity of the existing theories and techniques.

By the 1990s, multiculturalism had arrived in the mental health and educational professions. One can state emphatically that multiculturalism is the "fourth force" in psychology and education. It has encompassed all groups represented in the United States. The issue that we are now faced with is how will our curricula reflect this diversity. The other question of significance is how will we really include the many groups other than the few minority groups that have traditionally been researched. More important, whether or not professionals of color will welcome their White counterparts playing a co-leadership role in this multicultural movement is still left to be seen.

BARRIERS TO THE MULTICULTURAL MOVEMENT

Everyone is born with the capacity to be tolerant of people from different cultural orientations. However, the sociocultural environment can impose barriers that impede the development of cultural flexibility. Ramirez (1991) outlines three major barriers to the formulation of an environment of diversity: pressures to conform, prejudice, and oppression. In general all three are represented in the messages conveyed by the various institutions in society and in the family.

Pressures to Conform

Many culturally different individuals have often experienced much pressure to adopt cultural styles that are different from their own. They were encouraged to reject the values and customs of their cultures of origin and take on the values of the dominant society. Refusal to do so could result in tacit punishments, such as limited access to programs that aid in the empowerment of the individual/family. The pressure also comes in the form of mythical ideals, such as that light-skinned people are more attractive than dark-skinned people. The result can be feelings of inferiority by those whose skin color is dark. Such individuals can attempt to lighten their skin by using skin bleaches and so on. Likewise, reference to a southern or foreign accent being less appealing than a northern accent has led to feelings of insecurity, refusal to communicate, or pressure to change one's accent for fear of being ostracized. To say the least, these mythical ideals prevent everyone in society from respecting and benefiting from diversity.

Prejudice

Through prejudicial practices those who hold the power in society prevent those who are different from securing equal status. The powerful message is that if a person is different because of his or her gender, race, religion, and so on, he or she is not likely to attain the same level of success or goodies as those who are more alike. Prejudice can be very limiting and destructive to the development of a positive cultural diversity sentiment. This is because it keeps people separate and exploits the fears and stereotypes of individuals.

Oppression

Oppression is even more of an impediment than any of the above two barriers. It incorporates the above two, since people are pressured to be what they are not and are prevented from participating in the activities within a society. Exploitation and exclusion from societal events are also part of an oppressive system.

DEFINITION/CONCEPTUALIZATION OF CULTURE

Evans-Pritchard (1962) captures the true spirit of cultural differences in his representation of the Christian and Muslim faiths: "A Christian man shows respect for his religion by taking off his hat but keeping on his shoes, while a Muslim man in an Arab country will show similar respect by keeping on his hat and removing his shoes" (p. 2). Mosley-Howard (1995) and Frisby (1992) provided various definitions of culture. For the purposes of this book, *culture* is defined as a way of living, the customs, traditions, and attitudes possessed by a group of people whose outer appearances, culinary traditions, speech, fashion styles, religious worship, and overall socialization are all unique to their cultural upbringing; culture is in no way suggestive of deficits, but rather of differences.

By this definition of culture, it is evident that this multicultural perspective uniquely provides the opportunity for two persons from different cultural backgrounds to have divergent views without one being perceived as right and superior and the other as wrong and inferior. In other words, a multicultural perspective tolerates and even supports diverse views of mental health. Thus a multicultural perspective is not viewed from a White, male, dominant-culture, urban perspective. On the contrary it takes a broad view of culture, incorporating education, religion, ethnicity, language, nationality, gender, age, geographic location, and socioeconomic factors. Therefore, one's cultural identity is dynamic, since it is constantly evolving as the individual moves from one context to another (Pedersen, 1985).

THE MULTICULTURAL PERSPECTIVE—A FOURTH FORCE IN PSYCHOLOGY

With the coming of the fourth force in the mental health field, greater accuracy in assessment and treatment is expected. This is because behavior, in and of itself, is not meaningful, unless there is a link between one's behavior and one's cultural values. If we judge one's behavior without placing it in a context, we run the risk of projecting our own culturally learned values and expectations (Triandis, 1987). The relevance of a multicultural perspective in the shaping of our understanding of the learned assumptions makes for a better therapeutic relationship.

In the 1960s, when humanism became a third force in psychology to supplement the psychodynamic and behavioral perspectives, it was initially received with much ambivalence and trepidation. Today, it is widely accepted. In the same manner, multiculturalism has been a source of controversy and anxiety. Concerns from the dominant culture that multiculturalism is an area that they are not going to be able to hold a monopoly on may be the source of greatest anxiety. Whatever are the issues that currently prevail, those in the field of counseling know only too well that multicultural counseling and multicultural education (subfields of a multicultural perspective) are here to stay. As we move into the twenty-first century, this multicultural perspective will be the fourth force in psychology with which we all have to reckon.

2
The Need to Explore Alternative Approaches to Assessment and Treatment—An Ethical Mandate

AN ETHICAL CALL TO THE PROFESSION

The continued diversification of the North American society is creating a sociopolitical reality that requires the psychology profession to examine more closely how it is going to preserve itself in a growing multiethnic, multicultural society. If psychology as a profession is to receive acceptance from the culturally different, it must begin to demonstrate its ability, commitment, and good faith to contribute to the betterment of life for all people. This can be addressed in a variety of ways.

First, psychology has to confront the politics of its profession. Issues in assessing and counseling are not morally and politically neutral. This attitude has only resulted in the subjugation of culturally diverse people and the continued belief that culturally different people are inferior intellectually and are pathological. It is time that the psychology profession not be excused for its passivity in the rectification of inequities in the social system.

Second, as a profession, psychology must begin to examine more critically what constitutes normalcy and what harmful assumptions are inherent in the psychology training programs. In this book, I am forcefully calling for the inclusion of cross-cultural competencies throughout the graduate training of psychology majors. Chapter 11 discusses such curricula in great detail. In addition, the American Psychological Association (APA) ought to mandate that all training programs infuse such curricula not just in one course as is currently the case, but in every course. It ought not to be a choice anymore for psychology training programs to simply have a course in ethnic studies. The APA ought to make this an ethical mandate with an emphatic statement that if psychology students do not receive such training, they ought not to be given a license to practice in any state. In other words, the study of the culturally different ought to receive equal attention and a fair representation of their strengths.

Third, a pluralistic perspective in psychology ought to have at its center questions pertaining to the validity of the current theories and strategies in the psychology profession. This is obviously needed because the existing techniques and theories have been found to be at best outdated and at worst ineffective in working with culturally different families. Psychologists need to be more flexible and creative in their assessment and counseling styles.

Fourth, psychology programs need to be more aggressive in attracting not only a more equitable distribution of minority students, but minority professors as well. Culturally different students and professors can counterbalance the misrepresentations by offering a different perspective from the typical traditional Anglo Saxon version. Along this vein there is a need to shift research energies from the pathological, intellectually deficient, culturally different client to the institutions that serve as buttresses for institutional discrimination. Likewise, studying the positive attributes of culturally diverse families via longitudinal research projects done in a variety of settings must become a point of focus as well. There are many advantages to being bicultural and bilingual; yet few research studies seem to highlight these advantages.

Finally, it is critical to recognize that culture pervades the life of every person in one form or the other. Culture forces a vibrant relationship between the personality of an individual and the social context in which he or she interacts. As a result, the roles people play and the normative behaviors expected must all be interpreted from an ecological perspective, that is, through the culture in which they function. In other words students in training ought to understand that different ethnocultural contexts reinforce different behaviors. What may be deviant or anomalous in one culture may be healthy and acceptable in another. Since the United States is presently the most culturally diverse country in the world (Comas-Diaz & Griffith, 1988) American clinicians need to be more attuned to the notion that mental health services to ethnically diverse populations must be delivered in a culturally relevant manner.

PART II

CURRENT MAJOR APPROACHES IN ASSESSING CULTURALLY DIFFERENT FAMILIES

3
A Multicultural/Multisystems Approach to Intellectual Assessment: A Bio-Ecological Model

The psychoeducational assessment of minority children has received much attention and discussion from educators and researchers (Oakland, 1977; Oakland & Phillips, 1973; Samuda, 1975, 1976; Mercer, 1979; Mowder, 1980; Tucker, 1980; Rodriguez-Fernandez, 1981; Vasquez-Nuttall, Goldman, & Landurand, 1983). There has long been a relationship between minority children and special education as evidenced by the disproportionate numbers of minority and immigrant children "shackled" into special education classes. This overrepresentation of ethnic and culturally different children in special education classes has been partially attributed to "the indiscriminate use of psychological tests, especially IQ tests" (Cummings, 1984, p. 1). The IQ test has therefore legitimized the labeling of many minority children as "mentally retarded" and their resulting placement in special education classes. This situation is changing, however, since educators are faced with greater public concern about equity in education and also since administrators are faced with an increasing number of minority and immigrant pupils in the schools. The objective of this chapter is to examine from a practical standpoint some alternatives to traditional psychological assessment for school psychologists.

NATURE-NURTURE DEBATE

Among the most volatile issues associated with intellectual assessment in the United States are the interpretation of test scores and the use of test data for culturally and linguistically diverse populations. Implicit in the use of mental test data for educational placement is a Galtonian notion that differences in test performance reflect fundamental differences in intellectual endowments and that therefore subsequent educational intervention is appropriately matched to these underlying differences. However, the scientific legitimacy of this assumption must be questioned since judgments about "low ability" often parallel race and class differences.

The nature-nurture question has become one of the most polemical questions in psychology: To what extent are variations in intellectual performance due to genetic or environmental influences? Although there is little disagreement that genes and environment matter in intelligence, researchers are divided over the degree to which it is heritable. But even if there were consensus regarding the heritability of intelligence, there are other far more troubling issues that continue to keep the nature-nurture controversy alive. One issue has to do with the interpretation of low scores on standardized tests of intelligence in terms of genetic inferiority and the assumption that intelligence is a fixed and immutable characteristic. Despite the theoretical and empirical research evidence in support of the notion that intelligence is more than what an IQ test measures, the genetic argument endures in some circles. The other issue concerns the use of IQ test data in making educational placement decisions. Low scores on these measures are used as "objective" evidence for placing children in special education, low-track, or general classes. Unfortunately, as mentioned previously, these judgments of low ability often parallel race, ethnicity, language, and class differences.

In keeping with the theme of this book, I conceive of intellectual behavior as an inextricable biocultural phenomenon and argue for an assessment consistent with this conception. The chapter is divided into two sections. Section 1 begins with a discussion of cognitive capacities. This is followed by an examination of the role of the ecology in which individuals develop and express themselves cognitively, and finally I call for a bio-ecological approach to intellectual assessment. Section 2 describes the nonpsychometric measures within a bio-ecological assessment system that were developed by Armour-Thomas and Gopaul-McNicol (in press, -b).

COGNITIVE CAPACITIES

Over the past twenty-five years, numerous research findings have provided a very good understanding of the internal mental mechanisms responsible for variations in the expression of intellectual behavior. Terms such as cognitive abilities (e.g., Carroll, 1993), cognitive processes (Sternberg, 1986), and cognitive potentials (Ceci, 1990; Gardner, 1983) have been used to describe the nature and function of these cognitive indicators of intelligence. These cognitive capacities, as we call them, enable us to acquire knowledge, to reason, to remember, to perceive information through various sensory modalities, to retrieve information from memory, to make decisions, and to exercise judgment. Sternberg's (1986) triarchic theory makes allowance for information-processing mechanisms, experience, and context. This theory pays attention to the type of information-processing components that individually or collectively are implied in the performance of a task, the nature of the tasks—that is, the degree of novelty versus automaticity (experience)—and the type of contextual adaptation. Sternberg's theory has been criticized because of the inability to develop measures of intelligence that fully assess his model. However, one should not get caught in the trap that a theory's incapability of being be transferred to a test of intelligence in some way invalidates the theory. The viability of a theory rests in part on the accumulation of data that help to suggest the robustness, succinctness, descriptiveness, and explanatory nature of the theory which in turn enable improved decision making. Oakland (1995) suggested resisting "efforts that impose a need for a test to be developed on the theory as a litmus test of a theory's validity" (p. 23).

Ceci's (1990) bio-ecological theory is in many ways derived from the triarchic theory in that there are explicit considerations for componential factors, experiential factors, and contextual factors. However, the former theory differs foremost from the latter in that the nature of context is dramatically different and the role that knowledge plays is also dramatically different. In the bio-ecological framework the role of culture is far more pervasive. For Ceci, context shapes solutions to intellectual challenges as well as the perceptions of them. The bio-ecological theory is also concerned with information processing although it stipulates that the efficiency of such processing is a function of context both during the early development and later at the time of the evaluation.

ECOLOGICAL COGNITION

Although psychologists function as if the technology exists with respect to how culture is used in psychoeducational assessment, the empirical literature on culture in relation to psychoeducational assessment has yet to be embellished. Routinely, psychologists make diagnostic decisions without considering the possible effects of culture as mediating and intervening variables. Considering the effects of culture serves several purposes in assessment.

First, it brings to the assessment robust knowledge of the family dynamics of the child. Therefore, parenting, child-rearing practices, disciplinary measures, punishments/reinforcers, the language spoken at home, religious values, the resulting relationship of these points to the society at large, and their impact on the child are indeed rich sources of knowledge for psychologists.

Second, consideration of culture gives insight as to what the child is exposed to in his/her domestic environment. Thus a child's potential is more readily assessed once the family background is understood from a clinical perspective and once the child's cognitive learning style is ascertained.

Third, observation of the child in various settings (Ceci, 1990) such as on the playground offers interesting information. Thus the insertion of context into the testing situation would add to the predictiveness of traditional tests (Ceci, 1990). In other words intelligence is a multifaceted set of abilities that can be enhanced depending on the social and cultural contexts in which it has been nurtured, crystallized, and ultimately assessed. Ceci (1990) noted that when children were observed in familiar contexts such as their homes and in the company of familiar significant others, a heightened ability to perform the activity being assessed was found. Likewise, when young men in the English-speaking Caribbean learn to play songs on the steel pan after hearing them only twice, but those very men are unable to perform tasks in the classroom requiring similar short- and long-term memory skills, this is indicative of a mismatch between real-life everyday performance and intellectual functioning on IQ tests. Therefore there is a need to expand the notions of intelligence that have been developed within the psychometric and information-processing traditions. This is indeed necessary because individual differences in IQ test scores do not usually coincide with individual differences on the macrolevel forms of cognitive complexity such as ecological variables (physical setting or motivational level). The fact is that even among a group of children who are otherwise similar there can be important ecological variations that contribute to their ecological development. This does not mean that information-processing theories and psychometric measures are not relevant in the field of intelligence. However, these theories need to be expanded to include a more cultural-anthropological approach. The important point to note is that IQ is quite a labile concept and is quite responsive to a shift in context. Thus contextual influences on more complex tasks inevitably cast doubt on the current conceptualization of intelligence. It is wise to consider the research of others outside of the psychological IQ guild such as anthropologists and sociologists, who bring the richness of the contextual influences into the testing situation.

Ecology is an inclusive term used to describe the sociocultural context that promotes or constrains the deployment of cognitive processes in tasks that require the exercise of intelligence. The notion of the ecological dependency of cognition stems from a basic principle within Vygotsky's sociohistorical perspective (1978) that nascent cognitive potentials emerge, develop, and are displayed within a sociocultural milieu. Vygotsky's sociohistorical perspective has guided much of the empirical research on cognition and development (see reviews by Ceci, 1990; Rogoff & Chavajay, 1995; Sternberg, Wagner, & Okagaki, 1993). Researchers in this tradition have sought an understanding of people's "everyday cognition" by examining their thinking in real-world tasks, in multiple real-world environments. What is remarkable about this body of work is that successful performance on these real-world tasks seems to require the same cognitive processes or strategies that are used in the successful performance on standardized intelligence tests. Yet there is weak or no correlation between performance on both kinds of tasks. A more comprehensive explanation of the inseparability of context and cognition may be found in Ceci's (1990) bio-ecological treatise on intellectual development and Sternberg's (1986) triarchic theory of intelligence.

A BIO-ECOLOGICAL APPROACH TO INTELLECTUAL ASSESSMENT

The contextual theories of intelligence leave open the possibility of assessing intelligence across various cultures as long as the domains of knowledge necessary for intelligent behavior are equivalent in their meaning and structure, have similar attainment value across the cultures, and are experientially similar in regard to the operations required to access them (Ceci, 1990). For instance, it is quite possible to compare two culturally different persons on a similar task, for example, determining skills in soccer. Such a comparison is possible, however, only if each culture provided similar experiences in this domain and if the values associated with the task were similarly emphasized. Thus in many cultures, such as Caribbean societies, little emphasis is placed on sports and nonacademic tasks as a means of determining success. Therefore, in spite of the fact that a person was exposed to soccer in both that culture and an American context, it is quite expected that the American individual would be more inclined to value soccer as an art than would the person from such a Caribbean community. Thus one would expect that the American's cognitive competence in valuing soccer would be more honed through environmental challenges in this domain. As researchers are realizing, the search for an unambiguous biological or ecological explanation of behavior may be fruitless since the same behavior can result from the deployment of different combinations of cognitive processes interacting with different contextually specific experiences.

Armour-Thomas and Gopaul-McNicol's (in press, -a) bio-ecological approach to intellectual assessment is based on the work of Vygotsky (1978), Ceci (1990), and Sternberg (1986), who suggest a dynamically interactive relationship between cognitive processes and experiences nested within contexts that cannot be understood apart from each other. The authors take the position that cognition is, in part, a culturally dependent construct. This is because as human beings, we are born into this world with diverse capacities that predispose us to engage in activities within any given ecology. Our behavior may be described as "intelligent" to the extent that the nature and quality of experiences to which we are socialized require the exercise of these capacities in a given context. Therefore, the cognitive capacities required for intelligent behavior in one context may or may not be the same as in another context. The expression of these capacities through behavior may be different, because the socialization experiences within one context are psychologically different from those in the other context. Consequently, the expression of these capacities may reflect the context in which they were socialized. This line of thought has led us to conceive of intellectual behavior as an inextricable biocultural phenomenon and argue for a bio-ecological approach to intellectual assessment.

In some ways, standardized tests of intelligence are consistent with a bio-ecological approach. They all purport to measure many cognitive abilities which are indicative of intelligence and which many scholars agree are in part biologically determined. Test items do reflect learning experiences that are similar to the learning experiences common in some home and school contexts. However, a number of caveats must be made regarding standardized intelligence tests, particularly for children from linguistically and culturally diverse backgrounds. It cannot be assumed that (1) the cognitive capacities measured are the only ones of interest; (2) the experiences sampled on the test are common across populations; or (3) the concept of time has the same meaning across populations. As a result, at this juncture it is indeed pejorative to suggest that there is a resolution with respect to interracial equivalence on intelligence tests and equally injurious to conclude that one is brighter by virtue of his/her score on these IQ tests. The implication for psychologists is that until these questions are answered, the practitioner must challenge these tests and the test developers who attribute differences in cognitive ability tests to racial or cultural differences. In spite of all the extensive research in intelligence testing, the question that comes to mind is why has this lacuna in the testing literature not been addressed by the experts in the field. Existing tests ought to incorporate multiple methods that examine both biological and ecological factors. Thus the psychometric theoretical, statistical approach alone would not suffice.

On the basis of these concerns, I propose a more flexible and ecologically sensitive assessment system that allows for greater heterogeneity in the expression of intelligence. In short, I contend that other qualitative, nonpsychometric approaches must complement the quantitative psychometric measures of intelligence. The following suggestions are some ideas for assessing culturally different children.

Before administering an intelligence test, it is necessary to conduct a differential diagnosis. It is only after ruling out the following possible causes of the child's learning or emotional difficulties that a psychometric/nonpsychometric assessment should be done.

Health Assessment. It is important to review the child's school records to determine that all is well physically. In addition, ask the parent about the child's medical history. This is important to ensure that the child is not suffering from dietary deficiencies or any other ailments which can impede his/her functioning in the testing situation.

Linguistic Assessment. It is necessary to rule out any linguistic issues that may be contributing to cognitive delays. For example, perhaps the child speaks a language other than English and therefore does not fully comprehend what is being said to him/her.

Prior Experiences. It is necessary to examine any previous educational or psychosocial experiences, such as the child's learning style, that may inhibit or facilitate the expression of intellectual behavior.

Family Issues. It is advisable to explore what familial factors, such as a recent divorce, may be affecting the child's performance in the clinical or school setting.

Once a differential diagnosis is made, the important point to remember is that there is no single psychometric measure that taps the three interrelated and dynamic dimensions of intelligence—biological cognitive processes, culturally coded experiences, and cultural contexts. Therefore, any psychometric measure or an amalgamation of tests (inter battery testing, the process approach to assessment, cross battery testing) which emphasize a score-oriented approach should be used in conjunction with nonpsychometric ecological measures outlined in Armour-Thomas and Gopaul-McNicol (in press, -b) and summarized below. These nonpsychometric assessment measures ought to be given as part of the battery of tests to further gain an understanding of the child's potential intellectual functioning and his/her ability to function in other settings besides the school.

Family/Community Support Assessment

This is a questionnaire designed to determine what support systems the child has at home or in the community, what the child's previous educational experiences have been, and what language is spoken at home.

Other Intelligences Assessment Measure

Gardner (1983, 1993) takes the position that all children can excel in one or more types of intelligence. Gardner's theories of seven multiple intelligences share the view that the human mind is a computational device that has separate and qualitatively different analytic ways of processing various kinds of information. He provides evidence for what he terms "factors of mind." He maintains that there are many types of intelligences and not one as IQ tests claim. Gardner regards his theory as an egalitarian theory, and what is most important to him is not whether one child outperforms another on some skills, but that all children's skills are identified. For example, one child may have a propensity for interpersonal skills, and another may have a propensity for numerical reasoning. These propensities do not arise because parents exposed their children to situations and activities involving these intelligences, but because children have "jagged cognitive profiles," somewhat akin to the learning disabled child who does well in one area and poorly in another.

Of all the theoretical positions, Gardner's is the one most outside the family of traditional intelligence researchers. He came to his thinking partly because he objected to what he viewed as the domination of thinking about intelligence by a few theorists. Many have criticized Gardner's thinking, claiming that he does not examine the possibility that various cognitive abilities exist within each type of intelligence. His theory has been denied theoretical status by psychologists on the basis that it cannot be subjected to adequate testing. However, in certain educational quarters massive gains in children's intelligence have been used to validate Gardner's theory.

The other intelligences measure developed by Armour-Thomas and Gopaul-McNicol (in press, -b) attempts to capture two of Gardner's commonly found intelligences among culturally different children—musical and bodily kinesthetic. In assessing culturally and linguistically different children their other intelligences must be examined since the IQ test does not reflect all of the intelligences of an individual. Therefore, questions should be asked of the child, the parent, and the teacher that may ascertain the child's musical intelligence, such as What (if any) musical instrument(s) does the child play and what level of proficiency has the child attained—beginner, intermediate, or advanced? Furthermore, asking for samples of the child's musical performances, compositions, and so on will provide further proof of the child's level of proficiency.

In like manner, to ascertain the child's intelligence in the bodily kinesthetic area, questions such as the following ought to be asked to the child, the parent, and the teacher: What (if any) sports/dance/art does the child partake in and how long has he/she been a participant in such activities? Moreover, what level of proficiency has the child attained—beginner, intermediate, or advanced? It will also be necessary to ask for photos or videotapes of projects or demonstrations or to try to observe the child while he/she is performing the activity.

Interviewing several different persons (child, teacher, parent) is necessary to add reliability to the child's description of his/her other intelligences.

Item Equivalencies Assessment Measure

Cummins (1984) points out that when referring to concept formation, evalua-
tors must keep in mind that it is difficult for examinees to know similarities or
differences in objects if they had little or no experience with the objects themselves.
This item equivalencies assessment measure attempts to equate a child's cultural
experience in every item of every IQ test by matching the questions on the IQ test
to the child's culture. As such, the child's broad-based information repertoire is
recognized. An alternative would be to determine if these children can perform
comparable skills typical of their native lands and to describe in a more qualitative
manner their strengths and weaknesses with respect to the skills they can perform
in their native countries, showing the similarities between these skills and those
found on the traditional tests. For instance, Question 4 on the Similarities subtest
of the Wechsler Intelligence Scale for Children-111 (WISC-111) reads "In what way
are a piano and a guitar alike?" Many children from "third world" countries may
not have ever seen or heard a piano. Perhaps the cuatro, another string instrument,
could be substituted. The situation is similar for Question 6, "In what way are an
apple and a banana alike?" Apples are not grown in tropical climates. Perhaps a
mango could be substituted. The important thing here is to determine whether the
child knows the concept of fruits of different kinds. This idea of matching items to
a child's culture has been emphasized by Sternberg (1986) and Helms's (1992)
cultural equivalence perspective.

Many test developers have attempted to reduce or ignore cultural influences
on cognitive ability tests by constructing "culture fair tests." McGrew (1994)
spoke of the comprehensive nature of the newly revised Woodcock test of
cognitive ability. However, these tests simply are attempts to control the influence
of different cultures rather than to measure them (Helms, 1992). Even the Black
IQ test that was developed (R. Williams, 1975) was biased in favor of a specific
social class and regional group rather than Blacks as a cultural group. The
insistence that White American culture is superior and universal and should be
adopted by every racial group results in the devaluation of the unique and special
cultural values of different groups. Few investigators have studied what Blacks
and other minorities have contributed to this society apart from being used as
points of comparison on IQ scores. Lonner (1981) discussed four types of
equivalence:

1. functional equivalence, that is, the extent to which the test scores mean the
   same thing among different cultural groups and measure psychological
   characteristics that occur equally frequently within these groups

2. conceptual equivalence, that is, whether groups are equally familiar or
   unfamiliar with the content of the test items and therefore attribute the
   same meaning to them

3. linguistic equivalence, that is, whether the test developer has equalized the
   language used in the test, so that it signifies the same to different cultural
   groups

4. psychometric equivalence, that is, the extent to which tests tap the same things at similar levels across different cultural groups.

Butcher (1982) listed potential nonequivalent sources in cross-cultural research and emphasized that failure to consider these issues can result in committing the cultural equivalence fallacy. Helms pointed out that the culture bias with respect to psychometric equivalence exists because "European American values, customs, traditions and characteristics are used as exclusive standards against which people and events in the world are evaluated and perceived" (Helms, 1989, p. 643). Thus permeating every question of these IQ tests is whether the answers are right or wrong, with the correctness being determined by the normative White response. The more intelligent individual is the one who can apply Eurocentric rules most effectively and expediently. Therefore, those who see alternative answers because they do not have access to the Eurocentric worldview are penalized and deemed less intelligent.

Matthews (1989) reported an incident when two White prelaw students convinced the Law School Admissions Services that a Law School Admissions Test (LSAT) question had two correct answers. Although these two men were socialized in a White culture, they saw an alternative, more creative response than the test constructors did. Another example could be found in Gopaul-McNicol (1993). The author noted that many "lesser developed" cultures value functional responses over taxonomic responses because the former are in keeping with the normal everyday life for many groups. Therefore, when a child responds to "How are a car and a boat alike?" by saying that "you drive them," it is in keeping with the functional use of these items; it is not the taxonomic response that they are vehicles or means of transportation. Yet as Piaget pointed out, the taxonomic responses are considered more abstract and therefore representative of a more advanced form of cognitive ability.

Until test developers investigate the item equivalence on these tests, the lack of cultural equivalence on the IQ tests themselves cannot be ruled out as an explanation for the between group racial difference of IQ scores. Until test developers assess whether Black/African culturally laden cognitive strategies turn out to be more effective strategies for equal or better outcomes for predicting performance, then it should not be assumed that Blacks are less intelligent. A recommendation would be to allow expert representatives of various ethnic, cultural, gender, linguistic, and social-class groups to assist in the construction of the test items themselves. The caveat of course is whether these consultants have the ability to step away from the Eurocentricism so endemic in their professional environment.

Please note that this author is not asserting that psychometric tests are not relevant in the intellectual assessment enterprise. What is being asserted here is simply that test developers need to integrate ecological contextual factors into their thinking process. In other words, these other group information-processing strategies might be some sort of implicit unmeasured aspect of ability tests as well as their predictive criteria. In many cultures in the world, teachers and parents reward not always the obvious answer, but often more creative, expansive responses. Thus, an individual who is socialized to develop and nurture innovative, expansive, interactive and spontaneous thinking may find it difficult, when placed in a testing situation, to reconcile the Eurocentric world perspectives that underlie test construction. In many British colonized societies, for instance, a student's achievement is assessed not by multiple-choice exam questions, but by the ability to respond to essays, resulting in a more creative, integrative learning/response style. For these students multiple choice is viewed as simplistic and not as mature a way of assessing one's comprehensive knowledge (Gopaul-McNicol, 1993). Students who have to adjust to a more detailed way of studying in order to respond to the right/wrong multiple-choice format usually find this frustrating.

In general, different responses are elicited on the IQ tests depending on the environment in which the child was reared and depending on the culturally biased items. An example of a biased item is on the Comprehension subtests of the WISC-111: "What is the thing to do if a boy/girl much smaller than yourself starts to fight with you?" In discussing this question Helms (1992) stated that researchers (Gordon & Rudert, 1979) contend that Black children are taught that the appropriate response is to "hit him/her back." After testing Black children, I often try to ascertain their cultural experiences by interviewing their parents. In response to why their child may have responded in an "aggressive manner" to that question on the Comprehension subtest, Black parents often say, "My child cannot come home and tell me a White kid beat him/her up." It seems that when Black children in the testing situation hear "boy/girl," they think White boy/White girl, so they know they are expected to defend themselves as they are taught by their families. It is not so unusual for Black parents to teach their children to defend themselves given the racism in this society. The fact that the question recognizes the need to say "boy" if it is a male child being tested, as opposed to "girl" if it is a female child being assessed, tells us that the response would have been different had the examiner asked a girl what she is supposed to do if a boy hits her. Mothers often tell their daughters to never allow a boy or man to strike them. Thus a girl would have probably given a more aggressive response if the question stated that it is a boy doing the hitting as opposed to a girl. Likewise, it is expected that Black children's responses might be different if they think that it is a Black instead of a White child doing the hitting.

A caveat, though, is that it is not statistically possible to quantify cultural equivalence. However, powerful information can be obtained clinically. Thus, psychologists who consider themselves more than just psychometricians will still find this measure very helpful since they can clinically create a cluster of items that form the construct of intelligence for a particular cultural group. This cultural equivalence approach certainly also falls under the rubric of potential assessment.

Contextualization versus Decontextualization

While McGrew (1995) found that vocabulary is only moderately influenced by American culture, Hilliard's (1979) question on What precisely is meant by vocabulary? is a valid one which advocates for IQ tests have not yet answered. Words may have different meanings in different cultures. For instance, while the word "tostone" means a quarter or a half dollar to a Chicano, to a Puerto Rican it means a squashed part of a banana which has been fried. It is important to allow the child to say the words in a sentence to be sure that the child's understanding of the word's meaning is the same as that on the American IQ test.

The important issue here is that most vocabulary is contextually determined, that is, it is learned in everyday contexts rather than through direct instruction. Children accomplish this decontextualization by embedding unknown words in simple contexts. Armour-Thomas and Gopaul-McNicol (in press, -b) found that children who did not know the word meanings in isolation were able to figure out the words when the words were placed in a surrounding context. Of course, on traditional IQ tests children are asked word meanings in isolation. While this may be acceptable for children who have had adequate educational opportunities in adequate social environments, for children who come from educationally deprived environments, word definition without the surrounding context may lead to invalid findings of their intelligence, in particular knowledge acquisition.

On the Wechsler scales, the examiner can contextualize all words by asking the child to say them in a sentence. Credit is only given if the child (not the examiner) says them in a sentence.

Paper and Pencil on the Arithmetic Subtests

Arithmetic taps skill, memory, attention, and speed. In the standard procedure, it is difficult to tell which is operating. Potential testing allows the examiner to rule out which factor is operating. For potential testing on the Arithmetic subtest of the Wechsler scales, use paper and pencil and say to the child who fails: "Please use this paper and pencil and try to solve the problem." This response will fall under a potential score.

Test-Teach-Retest Assessment Measure

While Esquivel (1985) emphasized that "performance scales of standardized intelligence tests appear to have the greatest predictive validity for Limited English Proficient students, and may provide a more accurate estimate of their actual abilities" (p. 119), the nonverbal subtests—contrary to the claims that have been espoused—are not culture fair and are definitely not culture free. In fact it is "the information (direct experience) components of these tests that carry their culture bound characteristics" (R. Cohen, 1969, p. 840). Nonverbal tests rely on one's ability to reason logically, and it is in the very aspect of this logical thinking that the most culture-bound way of cognitive processing is carried out. In some respects these tests embody a more analytic mode of abstraction than the quantitative information components. This is because at times the task requires the individual to extrapolate and relate to relevant parts of the test items. Thus the manner of cognitive organization is relevant for successful performance on nonverbal tests. The Block Design and Object Assembly subtests are highly influenced by the American culture, and individuals exposed to such items will find the experience less novel and thus their performances will be more automatic for American children. Hence the tests will not be measuring the same skills across cultures and populations. Most children who are from rural areas in "third world" countries have had little if any prior exposure to puzzles and blocks. Sternberg (1984) emphasized that "as useful as the tests may be for within group comparisons, between group comparisons may be deceptive and unfair for non-verbal subtests" (p. 10). A fair comparison between groups would require equitable degrees of familiarity or novelty in test items, as well as comparable strategies. Sternberg (1984, 1985, 1986) found in his study that it was the ability to deal with novelty that was critical to measuring subjects' reasoning skills. Gopaul-McNicol (1993) found that other more complicated activities that also measure nonverbal abstract reasoning and visual integration, as do the Block Design and Object Assembly subtests respectively, and that are more relevant to the children's cultural experiences can be used instead. The average child who comes from such cultures is very handy and is able to help in constructing buildings, making furniture, creating a steel pan, maneuvering a motor boat, or cutting grass with a cutlass even though he/she has no formal education in these areas. These tasks are as or more complicated than putting blocks or puzzles together. Therefore, it would not be logical to label these children as delayed intellectually when they have honed other more complicated nonverbal skills. Evidently, their American counterparts are not labeled as deficient because they are unable to perform some of the above mentioned activities that these children can so easily do. However, these skills are not measured on the typical Anglo intelligence tests.

Gardner (1983, 1993) noted that the performance gap between students from Western cultures and those from non-Western cultures narrowed or even disappeared when familiar materials were used, when revised instructions were given, or when the same cognitive capacities were tapped in a form that made more sense within the non-Western context. Thus nonverbal tests have not been freed from their culture-bound components. Clearly the substantive information experience is still culture bound. Besides, it is quite common on the nonverbal subtests, for culturally different children to get the more difficult items correct after they have passed their ceiling points or after time limits have been expended. It seemed as if the children were learning as they went along, that lack of familiarity may have been why they did not do as well on the earlier items. Unfortunately, by the time they understood how to manipulate the blocks and put the puzzles together, it was time to stop those particular subtests, since they had already reached their ceiling point. Of course, in keeping with standardization procedures, one ought not to receive credit for items passed after the ceiling point has been attained. A recommendation would be to tabulate two IQs—one following standardization procedures and one tapping the child's potential as evidenced by summing all points attained even after the child has reached his/her ceiling.

The test-teach-retest assessment measure is only to be administered if you realize that the child was not exposed to these types of items prior to the testing, that is, if the child never played with blocks, puzzles, and so on. Then you are to teach the child and afterward retest him/her. For instance, on the Block Design, Picture

Arrangement, or Object Assembly subtests of the Wechsler scales, if a child fails the beginning item on both trials, teach it and give the test again. Give credit under potential if the child gets it correct. The important point to remember is that the exact procedures are followed as in the standardized testing, except that time is suspended, teaching is done, and potential scores are given after the child passes the teaching items.

In addition, please try to answer the following questions:

- How much did the child benefit from the training intervention?
- How much training is needed to raise the child's performance to a basic minimum level?
- How well did the child retain the skills learned in the training period?
- How much more training is needed to ensure that the child retains what he/she has learned?
- How well does the child generalize to other settings (home) what he/she has learned?
- How easily is the child able to learn other difficult problems different from what he/she has learned in training?

Suspending Time

The question of whether speeded timed tests are biased measures of intelligence for some culturally different children is another critical issue. The North American view that speed of mental functioning is a critical component of intelligence is an assumption that to be smart is to be quick. Many contemporary theorists (Brand & Deary, 1982; Carroll, 1993; Eysenck, 1982; Horn, 1991; Jensen, 1979; Woodcock, 1990) based their theories on individual differences in the speed of information processing. This assumption also underlies the majority of creative tests for gifted children. Sternberg (1984) argues that while speed may be critical for some mental operations, "the issue ought not to be speed per se, but rather speed selection: knowing when to perform at what rate and being able to function rapidly or slowly depending on the tasks or situational demands" (p. 7). Thurstone (1924) emphasized that a critical factor of intelligence is the ability to substitute rapid impulsive responses for rational, reflective ones. Jensen and Whang (1994) emphasized that "the more the retrieval process has become automatic through practice, the faster it occurs" (p. 1). Therefore, the greater the speed, the greater the amount of opportunity for practice. Noble (1969) found that children can be trained to increase their reaction time.

It is important to note that while speed of mental functioning has been associated with intelligence testing, it is well known that the ability to make snap judgments is not an important attribute of intelligence. Baron (1981, 1982) also noted that with respect to problem solving a reflective cognitive style is generally associated with intelligence. De Avila (1974) noted that assessing culturally different children via timed tests confuses the measurement of ability with measurement of aspiration, since little regard is given to children who are not culturally trained to work under timed conditions. Gopaul-McNicol (1993) found that most Caribbean children have difficulty completing tasks under time pressures because this represents the antithesis of what their culture dictates. On the contrary, slow and careful execution of their work is highly valued, so that even if the child is aware that he/she is being timed, he/she may ignore the request by the examiner for a quick response and may rather execute the work methodically and cautiously. As such, scores tend to be lower for such students on the timed tests which comprise most of the nonverbal subtests. Of course, there are some workers such as air traffic controllers who must make quick decisions as a part of their jobs. While speed may be essential in such situations, most of everyday life's events do not require decision making in the few seconds typically allotted for problem solving on IQ tests. The important issue here should not be one of total time spent, but time distribution across various kinds of processing and planning events. The practical point to be made from this is that students ought not to be penalized for not completing a task in the allotted time. Instead, they should be credited for successful completion of the task. Again, two scaled scores can be tabulated to compare how they function under timed conditions and how they function when tested to the limits.

Das (1985) noted that many American Blacks have surpassed Whites in the judicious use of their speed ability, especially in athletics and dancing, yet on speeded tests they do not do as well as Whites. The explanation must be in their familiarity or lack thereof with certain stimuli. Whimbey (1975) offered suggestions on how one can boost intelligence through training. When students of low and high intelligence were asked to think out loud while solving problems, a difference in processing speed and style was discovered. In like manner, when the examiner suspends time on all of the timed subtests and then gives credit for a correct response, this falls under the potential score. In general tabulating two scores—one following standardization procedures and one measuring the child's potential—should result in a more accurate assessment of the child's intellectual potential.

Thus this measure involves the suspension of time and the tabulating of two scores—one timed and one when time was suspended. While the recommended methods of administering and scoring these traditional tests may seem quite unconventional and not in keeping with standardization procedures, they are a guide for psychologists in tapping the potential of culturally different children. Reporting two IQ scores—one following standard procedures and one taking into consideration issues raised above—may be the best way to understand these children's strengths and weaknesses. If psychologists intend to serve children well, they should focus not on quantitative reports, but on qualitative ones that highlight all of a child's past and present cultural experiences.

Ecological Taxonomy of Intellectual Assessment

Proponents of the resultant theories question how influential the environment can be in explaining individual differences in memory, speed, knowledge tasks, and so on. For example, when an American Indian child has learned to develop speed by games such as a bow and arrow, the fact that he/she does not perform as well on the current speeded IQ tests in no way suggests that this child is limited in speed. Cultural taxonomies arise out of one's cultural contexts. Therefore one's cultural experiences and context are integral to the development of one's cognition. Culture dictates the amount of time a child will spend on a particular task. Therefore the people of some countries of the former Soviet Union, Somalia, and western Africa, who have to barter for food on a daily basis, tend to have a greater conceptual comprehension of volume because an error in bartering for a volume of rice could lead to suffering. Likewise, in many "third world" countries where there are no street signs, people develop a strong conceptualization of spatial orientation. Accordingly, one can infer that the development of a specific set of skills can only occur within a specific cultural context, in response to specific knowledge and experience. Thus the implicit assumption that attributes are constant irrespective of the context in which one finds him/herself is erroneous. The fact that an individual can perform one task very well may have little relevance for his/her performing equally well another task that obviously entails the same cognitive ability albeit in different contextual settings. This is because it requires different types of values of attainment to respond to challenges in different environments.

In light of the fact that we have veered too far in the direction of formal testing, and in light of these desiderata for new approaches to assessment, several researchers propose a more naturalistic, context-sensitive, and valid ecological mode of assessment (Ceci, 1990; Gardner, 1993). This is not merely a call to regress to a subjective form of evaluation. There is no reason to feel less confident about such a thorough approach since reliability can be achieved in these ecological approaches as well. In fact nonpsychometric measures that are based on multiple assessment instruments in multiple contexts have more ecological validity than do psychometric measures that were based on a child's functioning in a controlled testing situation.

This ecological measure attempts to measure skills and behaviors that are relevant to the context in which a child lives (real-world types of intelligence, not just academic type of intelligence). Therefore the child is assessed in several settings—the school, the home, and the community. Observing children's interaction with their family and friends in their most natural settings brings to the assessment robust knowledge of the family dynamics and cultural experiences of the child. The examiner should look for:

- the way the child communicates
- the way he/she socializes
- the activities he/she engages in
- the friendships he/she has
- the roles he/she plays
- the respect or lack thereof he/she is given by family and friends

In addition, the examiner assesses the child's intelligence by bringing some real-life experiences to the psychometric measure. For instance, if a child is unable to attain success on the mazes, take the child to a real-life maze situation and see if the child can find his/her way out. If a child who cannot find himself or herself out of a maze can maneuver his/her way out of a complex parking lot, we are left to wonder: Which test was better to tap this individual's intelligence? Even intelligence experts such as Wechsler (1958) and Binet and Simon (1905) defined intelligence as one's ability to adapt to the real-world environment. R. Williams (1971, 1980) emphasized that the very fact that a child can learn certain familiar relationships in his/her own culture shows that he/she can master similar concepts in the school curriculum, so long as the curriculum is related to his/her background experiences.

Stage of Acculturation

Assess what cultural adjustment difficulties the individual may be experiencing. This is because to some extent, most culturally different children undergo some change (minimal as it may be) at unpredictable periods of time.

- *Physical changes:* the individual must cope with living in a new place where pollution and other environmental hazards can be a new experience.
- *Cultural changes:* linguistic and social institutions are different and thus the individual has to adjust to these differences. The individual has to function within new social networks both within his/her own group and outside of the group.
- *Psychological changes:* the individual may experience an alteration in his/her mental status due to culture shock as he/she adapts to the new milieu. This is a period of psychological transition from back-home values to host-home values.
- *Adjustment:* the individual has adjusted to the new culture, but values his/her cultural mores as well. Thus he/she is bicultural.

Teacher Questionnaire

The teacher questionnaire can aid in offering information on various aspects of the child's behavior.

- What have been the child's previous educational experiences?
- Was the child ever retained?
- How often per week is the child absent?
- What has been the child's academic performance in math—poor, fair, good, or very good? What has been the child's academic performance in reading—poor, fair, good, or very good?

- Did the child participate in any supplemental instructional programs? If yes, what programs were they?
- What are the child's motivational and attention levels in class?
- How persistent is this child?
- How does the child relate to his/her peers?
- How does the child behave in class? In other words is the child reflective or impulsive?
- Is the child responsible? How so?
- Is the child disciplined? How so?
- Does the child prefer to study alone or in a group?
- Does the child prefer dim or bright lights?

The answers should all be written up in a qualitative manner in the report.

Recommendations

It is critical for clinicians to make recommendations commensurate with their assessment findings. Thus after doing potential intellectual assessment, you should recommend what you believe are the best ways in which the teacher, parent, or mental health worker can intervene in working with the child. In other words, if teaching helped, then recommend one-on-one teaching for a particular number of sessions. If extending time helped, then recommend that the child be given extra time and more opportunity for practice. If contextualizing words helped, recommend that initially as the child acclimates to the new environment, he/she be given an opportunity to receive his/her assignment in a surrounding context. If the child was found to do better on paper and pencil tasks than on tasks requiring mental computations, then recommend that paper and pencil assessment be allowed. If the child has other intelligences, recommend programs where these can be further enriched. It is also important to utilize all of the resources in the community— church, social/recreational community programs, after-school programs, legal aid, psychotherapeutic programs, and so on.

The important role of the psychologist is to assist the school-based support team, the teacher, the family, and the child to develop a course of treatment that would maximize every opportunity for the child to move from his/her actual functioning to his/her potential functioning in a three-year period. In other words, the child should show significant gains after the intervention period in all areas assessed.

CONCLUSION

In summary, it is not difficult to perform ecological assessments. There seems to be more a lack of will in doing so. It is hard to imagine one doing a comprehensive evaluation without such contextual experiences being seriously represented by judiciously observing individuals in more natural environments. This "assessment view" seeks to connect school activities with after-school activities with emphasis on the individual's strengths. In other words, this approach calls for a broader menu of assessment options and an abandonment of the sophomoric mentality that relies upon some type of rigid superficial conformity. We have witnessed a movement to render psychologists and psychometricians unemployable because of the limitations of these formal tests. A broader trained cadre of workers would make greater use of the many subsets of human talents by embracing this assessment approach. The question that one should always keep in mind is whether the tasks on the decontextualized intelligence tests bear any resemblance to the values held by the surrounding community. In that way, intelligence is really a flexible, mobile, culturally dependent construct. Many contemporary test developers still define intelligence as a unitary attribute with a cognitive overtone situated only in the individual's head. Most of children's learning is socially constructed in that they learn mainly through social interaction. Yet testing in most North American contexts is so formalized and looks only at the individual, not at the individual vis-à-vis his/her community. These tests require people to examine decontextualized tasks rather than examining how people function when they can draw upon their experiences and knowledge as they typically have to do in the real world. The extensive attention given to the cognitive information-processing components in testing situations is based on an assumption that the same processes are required to function in real-life contextual situations. Knowing about abstract analogies or about word meanings in isolation does not mean that one's human intellectual performance is adequately represented. It is amazing that we live in a society so advanced in technology, and yet we use numbers and scores as primary bases for triage. The ideal contemporary approach would be when standardized tests are only one component of a broad-based intellectual evaluation, in which interviews with parents and observation of children in their natural settings (community, home, school, etc.) would be equally valued.

4
A Multimodal/Multisystems Approach to Visual Motor and Educational Assessment

VISUAL MOTOR ASSESSMENT

The Bender Gestalt Test has been recognized as one of the most useful tools in the assessment of neurological functioning (Ghassemzadeh, 1988). It is an instrument which measures perceptual motor development, visual motor integration, and motor coordination (Sattler, 1988; Taylor, 1984). Since its introduction, many scoring systems have been devised for use with the Bender Gestalt (Hutt, 1977). Of these scoring systems, the most widely used is that developed by Koppitz (1981), which has been used primarily as a screening instrument for neurological problems (Eno & Deitchmann, 1980) and also for the identification of perceptual motor deficits.

Ethnicity has been found to relate to the visual motor performance of children (Connelly, 1983; Koppitz, 1975; Taylor & Partenio, 1984). Studies have shown that Black and Hispanic children perform lower than White children at almost every age level (Sattler & Gwynne, 1982). Unfortunately the studies do not seem to offer any clues to account for these ethnic differences.

Robin (1983) found that the performance of children from varying cultural backgrounds on the Bender Gestalt Test may be related to differences in the experiences that the children had prior to the testing. The author did not agree with previous investigators who felt that the delayed performance of culturally diverse children on these perceptual motor tests is a result of delays in their cognitive development. Rather, the author concluded that the delays can be attributed to the familiarity or lack thereof with these types of tasks.

Gilmore, Chandy, and Anderson (1975) compared Mexican American students' performance on the Bender Gestalt with that of Caucasians. The researchers found that at early ages (five or six), no significant differences were evident between the mean scores of the Mexican American sample and of the normative group. Beginning at age seven, a noticeable trend for the Mexican American subjects was observed. More errors were made by this group than by their Caucasian counterparts. The authors attributed these differences to the way the groups responded to the demands for accuracy, order, and conformity. The authors believed that Caucasian children learn and are rewarded for responding to these demands more than non-Caucasian students.

Gopaul-McNicol (1993) administered the Bender Gestalt Test of visual motor integration to West Indian and West Indian American children. It was found that most children made errors of rotation more than any other error. In testing the limits after the initial administration, these children were able to recognize that their designs were different from those of the original. Since on the Bender Gestalt, rotations are scored as errors, leading to the labeling of some of these children as neurologically impaired or as having visual-motor deficits, it is imperative to consider a differential diagnosis since the clinical indicators purported by errors of rotation and distortion may not be applicable for West Indian subjects. The fact that the children were able to draw the designs correctly once taught to do so suggests that there may be cultural differences in visual perception, rather than visual-motor deficits as many psychologists erroneously conclude. It is obvious that the present findings lend support to the fact that Bender Gestalt Test performance can be related to cultural influences and should be interpreted with caution for immigrant children. It may be necessary for school psychologists, when testing some immigrant children via the Bender Gestalt Test, to point out to the student any rotation errors noted after the initial administration of all nine Bender Gestalt designs. Allotting extra time for redrawing the designs is also suggested. This will aid in determining if errors are truly a clinical sign or a culturally different interpretation in visual perception.

Gopaul-McNicol (1993) also found that many of these West Indian children took approximately fifteen minutes to complete all of the designs. Even when they were told to work quickly, they continued to work at a slow pace. Of course, this may be in keeping with the cultural customs of these children. The social awareness that "anytime is West Indian time," seemed to fit the unhurried attitude they took when told they were being timed. Therefore, psychologists may need to encourage West Indian students to work at a more rapid pace and refrain from making erroneous assumptions about students' motivational attitude.

Although several objective scoring systems have been developed for use with the Bender Gestalt Test, each has been criticized as being inadequate in some form or another (Parsons & Weinberg, 1993). Neale and McKay (1985) claim that the Koppitz system is not as objective as is desired. They found that with the increase in number of raters for a set of protocols, the interrater reliability on an item-by-item basis decreased. In other words, raters had difficulty following the standard procedures set forth by the system, which resulted in disagreement pertaining to individual items. Brannigan and Brunner (1989) suggested that all elements of clinical judgment be incorporated into an objective scoring system—responding to both essentials of the Gestalt as a whole and the amount of differentiation between the designs themselves (Schacter, Brannigan, & Tooke, 1991).

Sugar (1992) developed a new, but as yet unpublished, scoring system which incorporates both qualitative and quantitative components focusing on remediating the aforementioned difficulties and which purportedly can be used easily by non-trained educators and clinicians. The Sugar scoring system utilizes six of the original nine Bender Gestalt designs (modified version) which are developmentally appropriate for five- to six-year-olds (Figures A, 1, 2, 4, 6, and 8). As in the Koppitz system, scores on the quantitative component are based on integration, perseveration, rotation, distortion of shape, distortion of size, and linearity. Scores on the qualitative components are based on the Gestalt of the six designs and on the strategies and mode of execution used, taking into account the number of times a child makes a qualitative error. A point system ranging from 0 to 1 point is given per design reproduction, with 0 points depicting failure and 1 point representing acceptable performance. A maximum total of 6 points can be obtained for the quantitative category. As previously discussed, the qualitative segment reflects overall Gestalt, strategy, and execution. A point system ranging from 0 to 2 points is allotted per criterion, with 0 points representing minimal quality and 2 points depicting maximum quality. After weighting of the quantitative and qualitative scores, a single score (which is an average of the two components) is tabulated, with a mean of 100 and a standard deviation of 15. Parsons and Weinberg (1993) found that this new system has been shown to be psychometrically sound in validity and reliability. Because the Sugar scoring system is more sensitive to a clinical perspective than the Koppitz system, Brannigan and Brunner (1992) and Parsons and Weinberg (1993) have recommended it as a better and more reasonable alternative to the existing scoring methods of the Bender Gestalt for culturally different children. Besides, it seems to have more applicability in clinical, educational, and research settings than the other scoring systems.

Gopaul-McNicol, Scully-Demartini, and Diaz (1995) examined the visual motor performance of seventy Hispanic children, ages 5:0 to 6:11 years, who were originally from Puerto Rico, the Dominican Republic, Ecuador, Colombia, or El Salvador. Along with the Bender Gestalt Test, two scoring systems—the Koppitz (1975) and Sugar (1992)—were examined to determine the best measure of visual motor functioning. Although this study is currently under investigation, the current findings reveal that the Sugar scoring system yields a higher score than the Koppitz scoring system. It is possible that the combined quantitative and qualitative scoring system allows the child the opportunity to interject his/her cultural experiences into the testing situation. Thus in assessing a child's perceptual motor functioning, a scoring system that takes into consideration the impact of culture via a qualitative approach ought to be a focus. Like in intellectual assessment, a unimodal approach (quantitative only) is not advised. Rather, a multimodal approach (quantitative and qualitative) with cultural considerations is recommended for greater accuracy in assessment and diagnosis.

EDUCATIONAL ASSESSMENT

In 1973 the American Association of Colleges for Teacher Education (AACTE) launched a forceful multicultural statement which read in part: "To endorse cultural pluralism is to understand and appreciate the differences that exist among the nation's citizens." (The AACTE's full statement can be found in the 1977 special issue of *Personnel and Guidance Journal.*) This statement clearly suggests that merely placating and accommodating racially and culturally different students is not what cultural pluralism is about. Rather, cultural pluralism requires educators to take a serious look at their curriculum, which has thus far only endorsed the principle of one model American and has not yet given intrinsic respect to every individual. Teachers should consider the strengths and learning styles of different children as remediation is offered. Dunn (1978) and Dunn et al. (1990) emphasized that if a student does not learn the way the teacher teaches, it is incumbent upon the teacher to teach the student according to the best way he or she learns. This is important because instruction in the typical American classroom is very visual, whereas many immigrant children are very auditory. Therefore speaking, rather than writing information on the board, or using audiotapes for instruction, rather than visual aids such as computers, may prove to be more successful approaches with these children. Another difference in educational style is the type of examinations that are given. Some immigrant children are more comfortable with essay tests, while multiple-choice tests are more common in the United States. It takes some time for children to get used to this form of test. Some children actually feel that the teacher will not take scores on multiple-choice tests seriously because, in their perception, essay tests truly test knowledge and multiple-choice tests are simplistic (Gopaul-McNicol, 1993). In addition, many immigrant children engage in a more cooperative type of learning, which fosters more dependence and sharing; in contrast, the American educational style is more independent. These differences in learning styles are critical; teachers must respect these differences and initially they should allow sufficient time for students to adjust and adapt to the American style.

Curriculum-Based Assessment

Over the past five years there has been much discussion around a serious need to examine alternative testing models in the area of education for determining the educational placement of children. A major limitation of educational achievement tests is their content validity (Shapiro, 1987). The existing achievement tests fail to adequately sample the classroom curriculum. Therefore these test scores may not appropriately measure what the child has learned. Shapiro (1987) found that there is a marked difference between the curriculum and the achievement tests, not only in reading, but in math as well. Another concern is the relevance of the test information gathered from the traditional achievement tests in planning a child's educational instructional program. The need for alternative assessment procedures to help plan instruction is critical if we are to best serve children—in particular children with special needs. There are statutory laws such as the Protection in Evaluation Procedures guidelines in Public Law 94-142 (Section 615-5C), which state that "procedures to assure that testing and evaluation materials and procedures utilized for the purposes of evaluation and placement of handicapped children will be selected and administered so as not to be racially or culturally discriminatory." The call for a more individual assessment procedure which is more capable of addressing the specific educational needs of all children has become crucial.

Curriculum-based assessment (CBA) has been proposed by Shinn (1989) to redress some of the issues in this arena. It is built on the premise that the measures are tied to the student's curriculum in order to facilitate frequent administration by educators. It is also inexpensive since CBA does not require the procurement of costly test materials. Another advantage of CBA is the ability of the examiner to engage in repeated measurement of a student's performance as the curriculum unfolds. As they stand, traditional achievement tests are normed referenced and rely on indirect measurement of student skills. Curriculum-based assessment on the other hand is based on a curriculum-referenced approach that indicates the student's level of competence in his/her local school curriculum. For example, the assessment of reading skills is drawn from the student's basal reading series, and spelling is assessed via the words that the student learned in the classroom. The relevance of curriculum-based assessment for linguistically and culturally diverse children is one of the reasons for the endorsement of this approach among educators. Obviously, it is easier to measure growth and progress in a student's performance. Besides, CBA can identify student curricular skills that may need further testing. Another obvious advantage of CBA is that it is not necessary to give an entire battery merely to determine an aspect of the child's performance, as is typical of assessing children with criterion-referenced tests. Certainly CBA is more time effective and more content specific. Furthermore, CBA encourages the examiner to become familiar with the child's curriculum at a given grade. Therefore, emphasis should be on an exclusive assessment of the task that students have to learn. Teachers can then develop their own instructional materials based on the results of the assessment (Hargis, 1987). In actuality, Gickling and Havertape (1981) pioneered the current movement of linking assessment to curriculum in a model best conceptualized as an accuracy model. CBA is indeed significant for instructional planning purposes, rendering it more of an intervention model than an assessment model as such.

Multisystems Assessment

An informal assessment involving behavioral observations in several settings—classroom, playground, the home, and, if possible, the community—will also help in understanding the needs, strengths, and weaknesses of the child before a referral to special education is made. Some children are quite capable of performing basic mathematical skills in a grocery store and yet on a structured test, they find themselves at a loss. Gopaul-McNicol (1993) noted that immigrant children who may not be as communicative in the classroom are able to negotiate quite well for themselves in the larger community. They are often more articulate on the playground in spite of the taciturnity noted in the classroom. When placed in a context such as the playground, they utilize words that they often have difficulty defining or expressing in the traditional testing situation. Therefore, assessing children in a multitude of settings is advised, particularly if the children are from diverse backgrounds.

Moreover, when working with immigrant children, it is also advisable to assess what their parents know or do not know about the American educational system. Teachers may need to set aside the time to educate parents on class programs, methodology for skill development, the purpose of study guides, homework policy, tests, the criteria for student evaluation, and what parents can do to further reinforce what is being done in the school. In addition, teachers must distribute to parents information pertaining to their educational rights and responsibilities, especially if the children are being considered for special educational placement. This information is succinctly outlined in handbooks for parents (Gopaul-McNicol, Thomas, & Irish, 1991; Thomas & Gopaul-McNicol, 1991).

5
A Multicultural/Multimodal/Multisystems Approach to Personality Assessment

While there is an incredible body of literature on the topic of psychopathology among people of African American ancestry, considerably less literature exists on its cross-cultural manifestations. In the mental hospitals, anxiety has been reported as the second most frequent complaint among children and adolescents and depression has been noted as the second commonly diagnosed psychopathology (Kashani et al., 1987). However, an intriguing paradox between immigrant status and mental health has been raised; although immigrants tend to report a high number of symptoms of psychological distress, when prevalence of psychiatric disorders is examined, immigrants tend to show lower rates of mental health difficulties than their U.S.-born counterparts (Burnham et al., 1987). Evidently, these apparently disparate findings raise concerns about the validity of Westernized diagnostic criteria for immigrants as a group. The third edition, revised, of the *Diagnostic and Statistical Manual of Mental Disorders* (*DSM-III-R*), like its predecessors, assumes that across cultures and across populations, people manifest psychiatric distress similarly. However, evidence from cross-cultural studies of depression and other mental disorders suggests otherwise (Marsella et al., 1973; Tseng et al., 1986). The *DSM-IV*, unlike its predecessors, attempts to address specific cultural factors endemic to cross-cultural populations.

COMMONLY ACCEPTED PSYCHOPATHOLOGICAL DISORDERS AMONG IMMIGRANTS

While many disorders are seen in many cultures, the manifestation and acceptance of these disorders are dependent upon the cultural values (Draguns, 1987). In general, mood (e.g., depression) and anxiety disorders are more prevalent and accepted than personality and thought disorders (Gopaul-McNicol, 1993). In most "third world" countries, repression of one's sexuality creates difficulties that are seen in a more psychosomatic manner such as vague physical aches, pains, dizziness, upset stomach, gas problems (mainly reported in the stomach), and nerves. Oftentimes these psychosomatic complaints are masking a depressive type of disorder that the individual for cultural reasons is unable to talk about. The reason that physical complaints are more accepted than psychological ones is most likely because most people around the world have not conceptualized psychotherapy in the same manner as Westerners have. The truth is that physical complaints elicit much compassion, whereas psychological complaints result in a sense of weakness and failure especially on the part of men. Thus secondary gains are often achieved if the person is relieved of his/her responsibilities because of these ailments. Generally the stresses include spousal abuse, marital tensions, infertility, the death of loved ones, querulous in-laws, defiant children, poverty, and the evil eye of family or friends. The response is usually in the form of physical and psychological symptoms that result in psychosomatic ailments, such as heart weakness, bodily aches, digestive problems, sleep disturbance, psychic dissociation, and hysteria. A classic example is captured in the vignette below.

Case Example

Mary was failing four of seven courses. She tried to no avail to explain the situation to her parents. They refused to respond to her concerns that the courses were difficult, and instead they said that she did not try hard enough. Suddenly she developed many ailments which were diagnosed as nerves. She was given Valium to address the "physical problem." This resulted in complaints of stomach aches, dizziness, and the inability to carry out the usual household chores and school assignments. Mary's parents were forced to address these physical ailments and were more sensitive to her academic failings. Mary, through these psychosomatic complaints, got her parents to respond to her needs and to be less harsh on her when she did not pass her courses.

Thus any cross-cultural study on psychopathological disorders would be aimed at answering the following questions. Can a direct causal relationship be drawn between an individual's culture and his/her symptoms? If the relationship is not causal, is there some other way in which the culture influences the maintenance and elimination of symptoms? The former question is difficult to answer as it has always been a compelling task in psychology to state with a high degree of certainty that one variable causes another. When an individual presents him/herself for treatment, the therapist is confronted with many aspects of the latter question. For example, In what way have cultural norms influenced when a person decides to seek treatment? What indigenous treatments exist for dealing with the pathology in question? Before addressing these questions, it is necessary to examine the risk factors that can lead to mental stress.

RISK FACTORS FOR THE DEVELOPMENT OF MENTAL DISORDERS

Immigration

Risk factors are those variables or situations which have the potential to make an individual or group of individuals vulnerable to developing a particular disorder. One potential source of stress for the immigrant client is immigration. For some, the very reason for leaving their countries and the means by which they had to leave result in traumatic reactions. The components of stress come from having to flee one's native country because of persecution, often abruptly, possibly with no chance to say good-bye to loved ones, with no opportunity to plan, with no means of bringing belongings on the trip, and with the constant fear of discovery.

Another considerable source of stress for immigrants, regardless of their reason for migration, is leaving family members behind. Sometimes anxiety symptoms are not even present until after the family is reunited. Having lived through separation in the past makes any future separation, real or imagined, a very toxic issue (Brice, 1982).

Once an entire family or individual has successfully left the home country, made connections in the United States, and established a home, other risk factors must be considered during evaluation and therapy. Adjustment disorder with anxious mood is a consideration when assessing reactions to a new home, a new physical environment, strange foods, and an unfamiliar climate.

Dressler (1985) has posited another risk factor for stress associated with immigrant status. He suggests that the immigrant's exposure to the American or Western lifestyle without adequate means to access that lifestyle can make one vulnerable to the development of symptoms. In his study he tests the hypothesis that the greater the gap between the lifestyle the immigrant is exposed to and the immigrant's ability to attain that lifestyle, the higher the level of belief in witchcraft and the supernatural. His hypothesis was supported empirically in two of the three groups he examined.

Family Role Changes

Unlike in Western societies, such as the United States, where nuclear families operate independently (Saeki & Borow, 1987; Sue & Zane, 1987; Triandis, 1987), in Trinidad and Tobago, the nuclear family is part of the extended family. To a large extent, relationships with neighbors and institutions such as the church and the school are perceived in a collective, family-like manner, rather than in individualistic terms (Triandis, 1987; Thrasher & Anderson, 1988; Gopaul-McNicol, 1993). Likewise, in Western societies egalitarian structures of power are nurtured and individualistic pursuit of happiness and fulfillment are emphasized (Kim, 1985; Sloan, 1990; Gushue & Sciarra, 1995); in the immigrants' native societies, however, individual desires are suppressed in favor of those of the family and even of the society. In many "third world" countries relationships are hierarchical and power is dependent upon age and gender (Gopaul-McNicol, 1993). Parents and elders are well respected in these societies, unlike in the North America, where youth takes precedence over the aged. Loyalty to and respect for one's elders are emphasized to the extent that it is disrespectful to discuss negative feelings about one's parents to a stranger. Moreover, children are socialized to focus more on societal commitment than on individual development (Brice, 1982; Gopaul-McNicol, 1993). An individual who pursues his/her own personal interest and forsakes the family's goals is perceived as self-centered and avaricious. Thus the self is defined more with respect to the roles the individual plays in the community and the family and less with respect ot individualistic terminologies. Because of this modus operandi, interpersonal and intrafamilial boundaries are not as clearly defined as they are in North America and the need for privacy is seen as selfish.

Family therapists often get referrals when the family has been reunited. Such reunification calls into question family roles and family loyalty. Minuchin (1974) has stressed the importance of maintaining optimal family structure. Every family has a structure which provides family members with a blueprint for how to behave and how to know what is expected of them. It specifies gender roles (male and female) and generational roles (grandparents, parents, children). Minuchin and other structural family therapists contend that when a structure is altered (e.g., boundaries between generations get blurred or members of one generation assume the duties of another generation), it gives rise to anxiety in the family. The precipitator for the change in structure, the gradualness or abruptness of the change, and the family's accommodation to it are just some of the factors which may influence who becomes the symptom carrier (i.e., the family member who develops a clinical disorder).

Racism

Another risk factor is the experience of racism (Brice-Baker, 1994; Gopaul-McNicol, 1993). Racial discrimination is something that immigrant and African American people share. However, there are some differences. Immigrant people of color have always been the racial majority in their countries of origin. They did not experience the lynchings, the hosings, or the Jim Crow laws that characterized the Black experience in the United States. What both groups have experienced is a definition of who is Black, which has been imposed on them by Whites (Gopaul-McNicol, 1993). For the immigrant a considerable emphasis is placed on skin color because one's degree of brownness has been so inextricably linked to social class. It is shocking for the immigrant on the lighter end of the color continuum to come to the United States and be relegated to the lowest rung of society. Anxiety can run high when one realizes that the lighter shade of his/her skin will not afford him/her any protection from discrimination.

COMMON MISDIAGNOSES AMONG IMMIGRANTS

Cultural factors play an important role in personality assessment. At my clinic, Multicultural Educational & Psychological Services, P.C., there were several incidents in which children's language was misinterpreted. A classic example is a child who referred to an "eraser" as a "rubber," which is the term used in the English Caribbean to describe an eraser; the school psychologist said the child was being sexual and promiscuous in the testing situation. Another example is when an immigrant child said, "I can beat him"; the school psychologist did not realize that the child meant "I can win the race" and instead described the child as aggressive and violent.

In assessing the emotional adjustment of immigrant children in the schools, it is necessary to examine the normal acculturation problems that any immigrant child can experience upon entry into the U.S. school system. In making a healthy adjustment to a new school, immigrant children will first tend to draw on their cultural background as a form of reference in the same way that kindergarten students draw on their home experiences. Many immigrant children, when they first arrive, are readjusting to their parents after several years of separation, since children are often initially left behind with relatives while the parents get settled and established in this country. During this period, children become quite attached to their caretakers, whom they come to know as their parents. When these children are reunited with their natural parents, conflicts arise around such issues as family relations, discipline, and culture. Conflicts also emerge when children are at different adaptation phases than their parents. Immigrant children can face overwhelming problems in school as they contend with the cultural clash between the norms of their country and the expectations in the host country (Goodstein, 1990).

In addition, immigrants typically come from homogeneous nations; they are accustomed neither to racial and ethnic diversity nor to the flagrant racism found in the United States. It is therefore common for them to experience confusion and cultural conflict. Several misdiagnoses can result because of these cultural clashes. Anxiety disorders, in particular posttraumatic stress disorder, depression, and schizophrenia are the most commonly found misdiagnoses (Gopaul-McNicol, 1993) and, therefore, these will be highlighted in this chapter. As a general practice, mental health workers ought to conduct culturological assessment of immigrant clients to avoid such misdiagnosis.

Posttraumatic Stress Disorder or Emotional Disturbance?

Due to natural disasters such as hurricanes and ongoing political unrest in many "third world" countries, many children enter the United States traumatized. T. Thomas (1991) has discussed the responses to trauma given the ages of children. In summarizing the literature, she stated that "the intrusion of memories and thoughts connected to the traumatic event can cause the child to be distracted from an academic task" (p. 5). Ronstrom (1989) found that some children become hysterical at the sound of loud noises. To compound the already stressful process of migration, these children are faced with memories of violence and death. The behaviors exhibited by children in reaction to these stressors can range from withdrawal to aggression.

Mollica, Wyshak, and Lowelle (1987) emphasized that in spite of the profound stress that these traumatized victims experienced, they have difficulty articulating their trauma-related symptoms, because the expression of the symptoms can significantly increase their emotional distress. The result can be poor academic work, behavioral problems in school, and more difficulty in acculturation. Unfortunately, these behaviors can be misdiagnosed as emotional disturbance. It is vital that psychologists allow children the time to acculturate and assist in directing families to supportive centers, where they can receive educational and psychological services to aid in the cultural transition.

Adjustment Disorder or Depression?

Recently, there has been an increase in referrals of immigrant children due to the "depression" noted by school psychologists. While it is important to be concerned about such symptoms as a lack of interest in social activities, feelings of worthlessness, and depressed mood, it is equally important to bear in mind the *DSM-IV* criteria for a diagnosis of depression and the stages of acculturation that immigrant children go through. Many culturally diverse children who are referred by the school for therapy because of depressed mood are quite social at home and in their communities. In most countries around the world, children are taught to be quiet in the classroom; North American school officials often misinterpret their respect for the classroom setting as withdrawal, shyness, depression, and so forth. Many immigrant children say that they are amazed at the liberties that are accorded children in the American classroom. It takes time for them to get used to this liberal, unstructured approach. Simply observing these children on the playground should aid in ruling out shyness and withdrawal. A more appropriate diagnosis might be adjustment disorder with depressed mood, since many of these children do not continue to show signs of "withdrawal" for more than six months (according to the *DSM-IV*, an adjustment disorder cannot have a duration of more than six months). With such patients, as opposed to those with more serious depression, the experience is transient, and suicidal ideation (if it exists at all) is likely to be anxiety producing. Helping the client cope with the anxieties and giving practical recommendations for dealing with life in the United States tend to have good results and to reduce the need for pharmacological treatment. In addition, reassuring clients that their symptoms are probably transient and that therapist and client together can alleviate them will be useful.

Religious Belief and Its Impact on Personality Assessment

In attempting to understand the causes of mental illness, many immigrants rarely invoke psychological explanations. On the contrary, mental illness is attributed to some form of spiritual restlessness meted out to the individual via a vengeful spirit. Many cultures have a belief in some form of witchcraft that can be worked on someone by an enemy to cause various forms of harm, usually out of envy or a desire for revenge. Folk belief says that when a person is "possessed," a spirit enters the individual's body, so that the behavior of the person becomes the behavior of the spirit. It is felt that the more suggestible a person is, the more likely he or she is to become "possessed."

Philippe and Romain (1979) found that females are more likely than males to become "possessed." These folk beliefs are deeply embedded in the culture and can exert a profound influence on people's lives. Many individuals wear a guard, receive spiritual baths (herbal baths with holy water), have a priest or minister bless the homes, or even throw salt around the house to protect themselves from evil forces. These beliefs are accepted by most sectors of society, transcending race, class, age, and gender.

Over the past ten years, I have seen several of my clients go to a spiritist while simultaneously seeking psychological help. For example, a woman had sought therapy because her sons had suddenly begun to misbehave "as soon as my mother-in-law had moved into the house." Since her mother-in-law had never accepted her, she attributed the children's misbehavior to her mother-in-law's "evil eye." She talked openly about her suspicions, assuming that the therapist not only understood but would be able to help her in exorcising the children. When the role of a psychologist was explained to her, she was very disappointed that the therapist would not even be able to accompany her to the spiritist. She felt that the problem with her sons was not a psychological one, but a spiritual one. Given the intensity of her belief, it was recommended that she seek the counsel of a spiritist first and then resume therapy afterward if the negative behaviors of her sons continued after the "bad spirits" were removed from them. She was receptive to this idea and more trusting of the psychological treatment process after she had taken the children to the spiritual healer.

Thus a therapist who hears a parent say, "My child is not conforming because an evil spirit is on him," and then sees the child wearing a chain with a big cross (guard) should neither be alarmed nor think that the family is weird. Similarly, when a woman attributes her husband's infidelity or lack of familial interest to the fact that "someone gave him something to eat that has him tottlebey [stupid]," she is not imagining something, but is expressing a cultural assessment of her husband's behavior. The individual who says, "I see the evil spirit in my house" or "The evil spirit talked to me," is not necessarily hallucinating, nor is the individual necessarily delusional who says, "God came to me and told me to give up my job, so I did."

If mental health professionals are not aware of the folk system, they may misdiagnose a client or devalue or demean folk culturological behaviors. The major point for therapists in assessing psychiatric problems in immigrant families is to try to determine the difference between "being possessed" and true mental illness. In dealings with immigrants, the area of most confusion is in the accurate assessment of schizophrenia, particularly paranoid schizophrenia.

To make a differential diagnosis, it is first necessary to do a thorough historical assessment of the individual's psychosocial, behavioral, and cognitive functioning. Schizophrenics often exhibit dysfunctions in thought, form, perceptions, affect, sense of self, interpersonal functioning, and psychomotor behavior. For a diagnosis of schizophrenia, at least two of the following elements must have existed for at least six months: delusions, hallucinations, incoherence or marked loosening of associations, catatonic behavior, or flat or grossly inappropriate affect. In addition, functioning in such areas as work, self-care, and social relations must be markedly low. Lefley (1979) found that the responses of "possessed" victims reflected little of the impulsiveness, lability, and free-flowing emotionality which characterizes schizophrenia. In fact, while "their consciousness is altered, it is not dissociated in the form of a split personality," as is commonly seen with schizophrenics (Lefley, 1979, p. 120). Schizophrenia is generally treated with antipsychotic drugs, which are useful for eliminating the delusions and hallucinations and alleviating thought disorder.

Many immigrants, while acculturating, may exhibit psychotic symptoms due to situational stress. Regarding the folk beliefs, it is enough to say that it is a pattern of social behavior which has been learnt (by constant exposure from childhood onwards) and in which people have been conditioned to believe. In other words, it is culturally sanctioned and is even considered to be a spiritually uplifting experience. "Possession is not abnormal, it is normal" (Wittkower, 1964, p. 76). For people who endorse the spiritual unrest view, the duration can range from one day to several years. The major point is that many people from culturally diverse backgrounds believe a spiritist can remove the evil spirit and free the individual from this "evil force." Therefore, whereas schizophrenics have difficulty eradicating the psychosis, the "possessed" ought not.

6

Best Practices in Report Writing for Linguistically/Culturally Different Children: A Bio-Ecological Psychological Report—A Multisystems Approach

Proponents of the bio-ecological theory (Ceci, 1990; Armour-Thomas & Gopaul-McNicol, in press, -b) contend that a more comprehensive theoretical approach involving the works of Vygotsky (1978), Gardner (1983, 1993), Sternberg (1985), Ceci (1990), and Feuerstein (1979) is very important in assessing students from linguistically and culturally diverse backgrounds. The modern Gf-Gc theory (with its emphasis on fluid and crystallized intelligence) is more concerned with describing the basic domains of intelligent behavior in the cognitive domain. With linguistically and culturally different children, their personal competencies (such as their ability to negotiate an environment that is highly different from their culture of origin), their many other intelligences, and their personal strengths must be assessed as well. While these recommended methods of administering and scoring traditional tests are not in keeping with standardization procedures, they certainly can assist psychologists in tapping the potential of all children. Reporting two IQ scores—one following standard procedures and one taking into consideration all of the child's strengths—is the most equitable way of determining the intelligence of a child. If psychologists intend to serve children well, they should focus not on quantitative reports but on reports that highlight all of a child's past and present cultural experiences. Table 6.1 summarizes the issues raised in Chapters 3, 4, 5, and 6. Before presenting a sample bio-ecological report, it is necessary to explore some issues in assessment/diagnosis and intervention.

DIFFERENTIAL DIAGNOSIS

With culturally different families, it is critical to conduct differential diagnoses for intellectual assessment, educational assessment, visual motor assessment, and personality assessment. Chapters 3, 4, 5 can assist the examiner in conducting differential diagnoses. For intelligence assessment, one must explore whether the

Table 6.1

General Reminders for the Bio-Ecological Assessment and Reports

The bio-ecological assessment must be done in the following order:

1. Do a differential diagnosis.
   a. Review school/clinic record—to secure the child's medical history.
   b. Teacher interview—ask about the child's medical history, linguistic competency, other intelligences, and teacher questionnaire.
   c. Parent interview—interview the parents at school or in the clinic. Ask about the child's medical history and other intelligences and conduct the family/community support assessment to ascertain linguistic competency, educational experiences, and family issues.
2. Assess the child's psychometric intelligence in school. You must have two scores: one for the standardized questions and one for the potential questions.
3. Assess the child ecologically by observing the child in the home and the community.
4. Parent interview—for further ecological assessment of the child in the home and the community.
5. Teacher interview—for further ecological assessment of the child. Observe the child in the classroom and the playground.

TIPS ON REPORT WRITING

1. When reporting the test results, put sections on
   a. *Psychometric assessment.* Even when you are writing the psychometric section of the report, your report should be qualitative. For instance, describe the child's strengths and weaknesses in the constructs measured by each subtest.
   b. *Psychometric potential assessment.* This section reveals the child's potential or estimated intellectual functioning. If the child showed an improvement in his/her performance, state so. Therefore, statements such as "Michael went from low average to average" should be emphasized.
   c. *Nonpsychometric ecological assessment.* In this section, you report on what you observed in the child's ecology—home, community, school. Discuss what the child was able to do in these settings and what he/she was unable to do in the IQ testing situation, even under potential IQ assessment.
   d. *Other intelligences assessment*
2. After you report all of your findings, you must have a diagnostic impression section and an educational/clinical implications section, that is, what are the implications of your findings for the child's functioning in the classroom setting.
3. Your recommendations should be based more on the results of the psychometric potential assessment findings, nonpsychometric ecological assessment findings, and other intelligences findings, and less on the standardized psychometric assessment intelligence test scores.
4. At the end of the behavioral observation section, please put the disclaimant statement for bilingual/bicultural children when you administer any IQ tests: "Since this test was not standardized on an Asian/Latino/immigrant, and so on population, the following scores ought to be interpreted with caution in keeping with the chancellor's regulations in assessing bilingual/bicultural children. Thus, these scores should only be used as a guideline in assisting school personnel in designing the best program for this child."

child's limited intellectual functioning is a result of mental retardation, educational deprivation, or a learning disability. It is important to determine why it is one and not the other. For educational assessment, in particular with linguistically different children, it is important to examine if the child's limitation is affected by linguistic factors. In other words, does the child have the skill in his/her native language but maybe not in English? Have you recommended that the child be assessed in both languages? This would help you to rule out if the limitation is a delay only in English or in both languages. To conduct a differential diagnosis for visual motor assessment, examine if the limitation is a cultural matter or a true sign of a neurological/visual motor disorder. Rule out why it is one and not the other. To do a differential diagnosis for personality assessment, it is crucial to examine whether the issue is depression, adjustment disorder, posttraumatic stress disorder, or a psychosomatic disorder. Again, rule out why it is one and not the other. Please note that with culturally different children, it is important to rule out cultural factors first (e.g., extra verve of some children) before diagnosing a child as having an attention deficit hyperactive disorder.

RECOMMENDATIONS

Your recommendations must be based on your diagnostic impressions after a thorough differential diagnosis is completed (Chapter 3 offers some specific suggestions). For achievement assessment, recommend the specific remedial programs. While initially the child may need the supportive environment of bilingual education, the goal should be to help the child become proficient in English. Self-contained special education classes are not the least restrictive setting. Explore other settings with other types of supportive programs first. With respect to visual motor, please note that a neurological is not needed if the rotations on the Bender were not truly clinical signs. Your differential diagnosis should guide you here. For personality assessment, you can recommend the appropriate treatment intervention based on your diagnosis. Please pay attention to cultural issues such as religion, family beliefs, role of family members, culturally prescribed ways of interacting, and so on.

Utilize all of the resources in your community: church, social/recreational community programs, after-school programs, legal aid, psychotherapeutic programs, and so on. In summary, you must be able to assist the school-based support team (SBST), the family, and the child to develop a course of treatment that would maximize every opportunity for the child to move from his/her actual functioning to his/her potential functioning in a three-year period. In other words, the child should show significant gains after the intervention period in all areas assessed.

Two sample case reports are presented below to illustrate the four-tier bio-ecological assessment system.

A BIO-ECOLOGICAL PSYCHOLOGICAL REPORT

Name: Michael   Date of Testing: 5/25/95
School: JHS   Date of Birth: 7/23/82
Grade: 6th   Age: 12 years, 10 months
Language: Spanish

Reason for Referral and Background Information

Michael was referred for an initial evaluation by his teacher due to academic and behavioral difficulties both at school and at home. Michael arrived from Nicaragua in October 1994 at age twelve. His parents had migrated to the United States when he was five years old. While in Nicaragua, he resided with an aunt and uncle, but had many problems engaging them interpersonally. His relatives in Nicaragua believe that Michael became defiant and oppositional after his mother left Nicaragua because an explanation as to why she had left was never accorded to him. There were reports of much aggression and disrespectful behaviors both at school and at home. Teacher reports reflect that Michael's maladjustment subsequent to his mother leaving Nicaragua could be a result of feeling rejected and abandoned by her, since these negative behaviors were not seen while his mother resided in Nicaragua.

The social history conducted on 5/16/95 by the school social worker revealed that since Michael arrived in the United States, he has had difficulty sleeping at nights. There are reports of him being nervous, afraid, and unhappy. His mother is concerned that he may be depressed. Michael lives with his two sisters, ages ten and three. According to his mother there is much sibling rivalry and jealousy on Michael's part.

Tests Administered and Test Results

Wechsler Intelligence Scale for Children-111

Psychometric Assessment	Range
Verbal Scale IQ	Borderline
Performance Scale IQ	Borderline
Full Scale IQ	Borderline

Current Scale Score	Range	Current Scale Score	Range
Information	Deficient	Picture Completion	Low average
Similarities	Deficient	Coding	Borderline
Arithmetic	Low average	Picture Arrangement	Low average
Vocabulary	Low average	Block Design	Low average
Comprehension	Deficient	Object Assembly	Borderline
Digit Span	Average	Mazes	Borderline

Wechsler Intelligence Scale for Children-111

Psychometric Potential Assessment	Range
Verbal Scale IQ	Low average
Performance Scale IQ	Average
Full Scale IQ	Low average

Ecological Intellectual Assessment

Estimated Overall Functioning	Low average to average

Other Intelligences Assessment

Bodily Kinesthetic (Soccer)

Artistic (Painting)

Family Support Assessment	Moderately low

Wide Range Achievement Test-111

	Grade Score	Percentile	Standard Score
Reading	1st	.9	52
Spelling	2nd	2	70
Arithmetic	4th	14	84

Bateria Woodcock Psico-Educativa En Espanol—Revisado

	Grade	Age Equivalent
Reading	4.4	10-4
Math	4.9	10-4
Written Language	3.9	9-6

Vocational Assessment

Interest Determination, Exploration, and Assessment System (IDEAS Inventory)	Arts/Crafts

Bender Gestalt Motor Test

Koppitz Error Score	8
Age Equivalent	Not scorable
Bender Recall	5 out of 9

Beck Depression Inventory	Clinical borderline depression

Vineland Behavior Adaptive Scales—Parent Edition

Communication	Low
Social	Moderately low
Daily Living Scales	Adequate

Social History

Human Figure Drawings

Tell-Me-A-Story (TEMAS)

Clinical Interview

Spanish Inventory

Parent Interview

Teacher Questionnaire

Language Dominance	
Spanish Expressive Vocabulary	Low average
English Expressive Vocabulary	Deficient

Behavioral Observation

Michael, a pleasant, petite young man, presented himself in a cooperative, compliant manner. He had a good disposition and was motivated to do all of the tasks assigned to him. Even upon completion of the testing, Michael asked the examiner if he could do more. He was not fatigued and saw these tests as reinforcing to him. In general his response time was slow and he approached the testing in a cautious, reflective manner. When he clearly did not know the answer he still persisted, but became noticeably frustrated and embarrassed. He would sigh, frown, and seem upset that he did not know the answer to what he initially perceived as easy. All in all, it was a pleasure testing Michael because he tried hard and was willing to please.

Language Assessment

Michael's language proficiency was tested through the administration of the Vocabulary subtest of the WISC-111 in both Spanish and English. He is clearly more dominant and more proficient in Spanish. He only spoke in Spanish and requested that the examiner speak only in Spanish. Interestingly, when he engaged in social play with two of his peers after the evaluation, he responded to them in English and they only spoke to him in English. Thus Michael has some English skills, but is too self-conscious to speak for fear of "saying it wrong." Michael's articulation in English was poor and unclear. On a few occasions it was necessary to ask him to repeat what he was saying. His English receptive skills were also less developed than his Spanish receptive skills. At this time, since Michael's primary language is

Spanish, the supportive environment of a bilingual class is recommended. Such a class would aid in his understanding and would enhance learning. Likewise, Michael needs to be evaluated bilingually.

Another Example of Language Assessment

Michael's receptive skills are stronger than his expressive skills, since he had more difficulty expressing verbal ideas than understanding what was said to him. Receptively and expressively he is more dominant in Spanish, since he only responded in Spanish even when the examiner spoke to him in English. Of note is that Michael is also more proficient in English since he was better able to perform mathematical computations in English and to read and write in English. He counted up to three in Spanish and knew some of the letters in Spanish. In English, however, he was able to construct sentences and to do applied mathematical problems. It is possible, since he only receives instruction in the classroom in English, that his English skills far surpass his Spanish skills in spite of his being more socially dominant in his native language. Because the Spanish translation improved his score in all verbal areas, Michael requires the supportive environment of bilingual instruction and ought to be evaluated bilingually when tested psychologically, educationally, and linguistically.

Given the fact that Michael is bilingual and that a Latino/Hispanic population was not used as part of the standardization sample, in keeping with the chancellor's regulations, the following scores ought to be interpreted with caution and should only be used as a guide for school personnel. The results should be interpreted from both a biological and contextual approach.

Psychometric Assessment

On the Wechsler Intelligence Scale for Children-111, Michael obtained a full-scale IQ score which placed him in the borderline range of intelligence. His verbal and nonverbal scores fell in the borderline and low average ranges respectively.

Subtest analysis indicates considerable subtest variability both within the verbal and nonverbal spheres. In the verbal area (crystallized), Michael was deficient in general information, suggesting that on this psychometric test, Michael is not as alert to the social and cultural factors so typical of American society as measured by the WISC-111. His deficiency in comprehension is also indicative of Michael's limited understanding of the social mores here in the United States as assessed on the WISC-111. Michael was also deficient in verbal abstract reasoning, suggesting that, on this test, Michael has difficulty placing objects and events together in a meaningful group. In arithmetic and vocabulary, Michael was low average. This is indicative of inadequate arithmetic skills on the WISC-111, as well as poor language development and limited word knowledge as defined by the WISC-111. In auditory short-term memory, Michael was average. Therefore one can expect Michael to be relatively good at rote memory and sequential processing.

In the nonverbal area (fluid intelligence), Michael was low average in identifying essential missing elements from a whole, suggesting delayed visual alertness, visual discrimination, and long-term visual memory on the Wechsler scales. In visual integration, Michael was borderline, suggesting limited perceptual skills, poor long-term visual memory, and limited constructive ability commensurate with his age peers nationwide on the Wechsler scales. However, Michael was persistent and tried to put the puzzles together. There was a sense that he was unfamiliar with these items. When he was taught how to connect the pieces, he tended to be more relaxed, although he continued to perform poorly. In visual motor coordination/motor speed, Michael was also borderline, suggesting slow response time, poor visual short-term memory, and limited visual acuity. In nonverbal comprehension, Michael was low average, suggesting a delayed ability to anticipate the consequences of his actions, to plan, and to organize ahead of time on the WISC-111. In nonverbal abstract reasoning, Michael was also low average, suggesting below average ability to perceive, analyze, and synthesize blocks on the Wechsler scales.

Another Example of Psychometric Assessment

For those who opt to interpret this test via the Gf-Gc factors, write a paragraph on each of the nine abilities (McGrew, 1994). For example:

> Processing Speed (GS) (coding) was found to be borderline. This suggests that Michael may experience difficulty performing automatic cognitive tasks quickly.
> Visual Processing (GV) (block design and object assembly) was average. This suggests that Michael has the ability to analyze, synthesize, and think with visual patterns. His strength clearly is his ability to manipulate visual shapes, especially those that are figural and geometric in nature. Therefore it is not surprising that Michael demonstrates exceptional talent in painting.

Psychometric Potential Assessment

When Michael was tested to the limits, when he was not placed under time pressure, and when item equivalencies were done, his score improved by six IQ points in the verbal area and five IQ points in the nonverbal area. Thus when Michael was asked to perform skills comparable to the puzzles on the Wechsler scales, he went from borderline to low average. Likewise, when the vocabulary words were contextually determined—that is, the words were placed in a surrounding context ("Michael migrated to the United States recently," instead of the word "migrate" used in isolation)—Michael went from low average to average. Since vocabulary is the best measure of general intelligence, Michael is of average potential in the verbal area. Likewise, when Michael was allowed to use paper and pencil on the arithmetic subtest, he went from low average to average. A total increment of nine scale points in the verbal area and nine scale points in the nonverbal area resulted in an overall IQ increment of eleven scale points, placing him in the low average range instead of the borderline range, as happened when standard procedures were followed.

In the nonverbal area, Michael went from low average to average on the Block Design subtest when he was taught (test-teach-retest) to manipulate the blocks. Thus again, Michael is of average potential in the nonverbal area since Block Design is the best measure of nonverbal intelligence on the Wechsler scales. Overall Michael's potential is at least low average.

Other Examples of Psychometric Potential Assessment

Example 1—item equivalency in the nonverbal area. The Block Design and Object Assembly subtests are highly influenced by American culture. When Michael was assessed by other, more comparable measures such as building a chair, he was found to be very superior given the quick and accurate manner in which he executed the task.

Example 2. Likewise, while Michael was unable to name two American coins, he was able to correctly name and identify the escudo and the peso, two monetary units from Chile.

Example 3. In the same manner, while Michael did not know who discovered America or who Christopher Columbus was, he knew that Pedro De Valdivia founded Santiago. Thus it is expected that if given time to acclimate to this society, Michael will learn American history and concepts to result in a higher intellectual functioning.

Example 4. On the Block Design subtests, Michael got the more difficult items correct after he passed his ceiling point or after time limits had been expended. In his native country, blocks and puzzles are not games commonly played by children. As such, he was never exposed to block building. It seemed as if he was learning as he went along, that lack of familiarity and ultimately anxiety may have been why he did not do as well on the earlier items. As a result two IQs were tabulated—one following standardization procedures and one tapping his potential as evidenced by summing all points attained even after he had reached his point of discontinuation.

Example 5. When Michael was asked, "In what way are an apple and a banana alike?" he did not know the answer. Interestingly when asked how a mango and a banana are alike, he got it correct. The important thing here is that he knew the concept of fruits.

Example 6. Also of note is that while Michael did not know the word "migrate" in isolation, he knew it when used in a sentence. Thus if words were contextualized, Michael's word knowledge and ability to express verbal ideas at varying degrees of abstraction was much higher. In the same manner, while Michael was unable to articulate how a wheel and a ball were alike, he was able to draw how they were both alike and then to state that they were both round. It seems as if he had to first conceptualize their similarity via visual stimuli, then to form the concept of sameness, before being able to express the common factor between these two objects. Therefore, it is not that Michael has not conceptualized this relationship, but rather that he has to go through a longer process in order to retrieve and articulate the similarity of such a concept.

Example 7. When Spanish dialectical terminologies were utilized, Michael was able to respond to questions previously misunderstood or unanswered. Thus while he did not understand the question "Why do you recycle paper?" he was able to respond appropriately to "Why do you separate paper in a separate garbage can?" Likewise, while Michael did not understand the question "Why do games have rules?" he clearly was able to produce a two-point response when asked "Why are rules needed to play marbles?" Thus merely rewording the directions helped with understanding and resulted in an increase of ten points.

Example 8. When standardization procedures were not followed, Michael's potential demonstrated an eight-point difference. For instance, instead of being presented for five seconds as in the standard procedure, visual stimuli or the Gestalt was shown for ten seconds (fifteen seconds for more complicated Gestalts), and word or number sentences were slowly repeated. This process resulted in the ability to process information, increase concentration, decrease anxiety, and correctly respond. This suggests that when given more time to process and practice learned problem-solving skills, he can perform quite better.

Example 9. While initially Michael did not understand the Block Design subtest, when a test-teach-retest technique was used (that is, when he was taught how to build blocks and puzzles other than those used on the Wechsler scales and was then tested again), he was able to correctly synthesize the more difficult items, to correctly strategize, and to respond to two out of three previously incorrect questions. Thus with respect to nonverbal abstract reasoning, he is more average than borderline as was seen when standard procedures were followed. This also shows that Michael is capable of learning various tasks once they are explained and he is given the opportunity to practice the tasks.

Nonpsychometric Ecological Assessment

Of note is that Michael had difficulty on the Mazes subtest (borderline). However when Michael had to direct the examiner to drive him home, and the examiner made a wrong turn, Michael was quickly able to maneuver his way out of a rather complex geographic location. He certainly manifested much intelligence as he located the route. He showed good planning ability and good perceptual organization when placed in a real-life situation. His low average to average intellectual ability was indeed evident from an ecological perspective.

Another Example of Nonpsychometric Ecological Assessment

Observation of the child in various settings, such as on the playground or in his/her community, offers interesting information. Although Michael had difficulty putting the puzzles together on the WISC-111, at home Michael had no difficulty dismantling a fan and putting it back together in a one-hour period. Thus when he was exposed to a more familiar stimulus, he was able to integrate parts into a meaningful whole, a skill characteristic of the Object Assembly subtest of the Wechsler scales.

Other Intelligences Assessment

Michael is described as very athletic, in particular in soccer. In spite of his small frame, his mother feels that he has a well-developed sense of timing, coordination, and rhythm when he plays soccer. Thus with respect to his kinesthetic ability, he seems to be average to above average in his ability to play soccer. Michael also has an affinity for drawing and painting. He was able to do cartoonlike drawings. His teacher mentioned that he was the best student in his class in art and related fields such as designing things.

More Examples of Other Intelligences Assessment

Example 1—musical intelligence. In spite of Michael's deficiencies in the verbal area, he is able to formulate melodic, rhythmic, and harmonic images into elaborate ideas although he never studied music. For instance, he plays the steel pan, the piano, and the cuatro without sheet music and with much fluency. He also composes music so creatively that in the realm of musical intelligence he would be considered superior.

Example 2. According to Michael's parents, he is very musical and plays the guitar for various Hispanic events.

Example 3—bodily-kinesthetic intelligence. Michael is able to dance energetically. His dances allow one an opportunity to observe his bodily intelligence in its purest form with much flexibility and high technical proficiency. He is indeed of superior ability in this area.

Example 4. Michael is athletic and is able to excel in grace, power, speed, accuracy, and teamwork. His ability to pitch the ball shows his analytic power and resourcefulness. Also noted was his ability to remain poised under great pressure. A well-developed sense of timing, coordination, and rhythm result in his being well executed and powerful in his gross and fine motor motions. His kinesthetic strength is indeed superior.

Example 5. Michael has an adequate amount of social competence to deal with issues in his community. For instance, he knows which areas in his neighborhood are drug infested and how to avoid going there. He repeatedly said, "Here is where the drug people hang out, so don't go there." He also knew that it was unsafe to flash money around and cautioned the examiner about opening her wallet even in the supermarket.

Visual Motor Assessment

The borderline performance noted in visual motor coordination on the Wechsler scales was also seen on the unstructured Bender test of visual motor coordination. Michael's performance was severely delayed due to seven errors of rotation and one error of integration. It seems that Michael had difficulties in both the conceptualization of the visual impressions as well as visual perception itself. Thus he not only perceived the Gestalts incorrectly, but also interpreted them in a concrete way to fit his realm of experience at this time. Besides, the designs were executed in a disorganized manner.

Like auditory short-term memory which was average, visual memory was also average since Michael recalled five of the nine designs. This suggests that remediation should be undertaken both auditorily as well as visually. Therefore audiotapes as well as computer aids would prove beneficial in remediating Michael in his areas of weakness. His figure drawings showed timidity and anxiety.

Achievement Testing

Michael was found to be on a fourth-grade level in Spanish reading, but a first-grade level in English reading. In math he was on a fourth-grade level in both English and Spanish. In spelling, Michael was on a third-grade level in Spanish and a second-grade level in English. Thus he is delayed in his native language in all areas, but is severely delayed in English. Because he has only been residing in the United States for seven months, it is expected that his English skills are going to be limited. With respect to his limited Spanish skills, it must be reiterated that Michael was not attending school for two years in Nicaragua when he was expelled from school at age ten. Thus in effect, Michael received education up to a fourth-grade level in his native country. His skills are therefore commensurate with his actual educational experiences. Therefore this child's prognosis for functioning at a higher educational level is good if he receives intensive instruction in all academic areas.

Vocational Assessment

Michael's scores on the IDEAS inventory, the other intelligences questionnaire, and the clinical interview point to areas of arts and crafts which he finds most enjoyable and in which he may find the greatest satisfaction. He enjoys making pottery and painting and is said to be very artistic in his ability to draw pictures of people, places, and scenery. Given Michael's intellectual potential and achievement functioning, his professional interest is commensurate with ability. However, career awareness and career exploration are needed as Michael moves on to high school.

More Examples of Vocational Assessment

Example 1. Michael expressed a desire to become a carpenter or a construction worker. He seems to know much of the trade and says that he likes to work with wood and to help his uncle install doors, windows, and cabinets and to do molding. He stated that while residing in Nicaragua, on several occasions he watched the complete building of a house. It was clear to the examiner that he had exposure to construction work in his native country. Career guidance is needed in this area. Furthermore it would be most beneficial to infuse a motivating factor in Michael's high school career. For instance, work study or after-school projects such as part-time apprenticeships would serve to mitigate some of the apathy seen during this evaluation. This is important for Michael, who sees himself as much as a student as an employee. Math skills of the classroom can be related to the math skills necessary to work with blueprints. Listening to instructions in the classroom can be related to working from the instructions of his supervisors in relation to a layout and in relation to local building codes and their dictates.

Example 2. Michael should review the Occupational Outlook Handbook and get a clear picture of the present and future prerequisites and criteria which he must attain in order to become a construction worker, enter the military, or have access to government jobs. He should also be taught how to be self-employed through the private sector.

Example 3. Michael should also be taught how to acquire and develop interpersonal and intrapersonal communications skills, which are essential to, or indirectly related to, a job situation. The starting point for this exercise would be the development of interview skills, such as practices in role-modeling situations. Understanding of how people's personalities vary and affect their working with others should be demonstrated, observed, and discussed in relation to Michael's peers, teachers, siblings, parents, and employers.

Example 4. Classroom and counseling activities should include writing a business letter such as those used in draft application letters and letters of inquiry. Moreover, how to prepare a personal data sheet would be another important activity. Vocational counseling, career guidance, and career exploration will all be beneficial at this time.

Personality Assessment

The personality tests, the clinical interview, and parental interview depict Michael's adjustment as variable. On the one hand he is a pleasant, charming, delightful, motivated, and sensitive youngster. He is interested in learning and wants to be a police officer. These positive behaviors are seen mainly in a one-on-one situation. On the other hand, the personality tests and the teacher behavior checklist reveal a young man who is angry and relates aggressively to his peers. Michael has reportedly hit, pushed, and physically attacked his classmates. He has few friends in class with whom he is able to engage interpersonally. Even children who are from similar cultural backgrounds have difficulty interacting with him. These behaviors were also noted in his native country, leading to his eventual dismissal from school at the age of ten.

Michael also expressed anger to the examiner as he recounted being abandoned by his mother for five years when she emigrated to the United States. He is resentful that he was left behind even though his sister was left back with him. He is intensely jealous of his younger sisters and feels that he is not as loved as they are. The clinical borderline depression score noted on the Beck does not indicate that he is clinically depressed as such, but that he has turned his anger inward and is experiencing psychosomatic ailments such as headaches and sleep disturbance. The underlying issue is one of much frustration, anger, and insecurity with respect to being loved and the desire on his part to receive more nurturing from his mother and stepfather. He has little communication with his stepfather and there is much guilt on his mother's part with respect to leaving him in Nicaragua. These issues on the part of both mother and son ought to be resolved in family counseling. Family support is moderately low since Michael's mother was not formally educated herself and does not seem to know how to assist Michael as he acclimates to this society. Family counseling should also empower the family by referring them to community support systems such as a church, or an after-school program so that the family will be assisted in their acculturation process. Individual counseling should also focus on building Michael's self-esteem and self-confidence and helping him cope with being different in his physical appearance. Michael is physically smaller than his male counterparts, and this also affects his self-image. Anxiety reduction training with respect to failing and being "not as smart" should also be provided via counseling.

Other Examples of Personality Assessment

Example 1. The stories elicited from the TEMAS indicate that his aspirations seem to center around survival themes and being able to cope with feelings of anger and fear. His style of relating to his peers is poor, perhaps a reflection of poor opportunities to socialize and/or inability to effectively express his feelings and needs.

Example 2. The current assessment also indicates that one major barrier to Michael's process of learning is his tendency to periodically withdraw and tune out. He is also likely to be highly distractible both by inner as well as outer stimuli. This tendency to withdraw precludes him from concentrating and paying attention, making it difficult for him to benefit from the instruction that is presented.

Example 3. Positive reinforcement and encouragement are likely to be effective motivational techniques, given Michael's strong need for approval.

Educational Implications

Michael is delayed in general information, comprehension, vocabulary, arithmetic, and verbal abstract reasoning. As a result, remediation should focus on exposure to a broad range of everyday facts, practical reasoning in social situations, and word building. Michael should be encouraged to read American literature or the newspaper on a daily basis, to gain more insight into world events and the mainstream cultural views and to improve in general information. Other resources are museums, educational television shows, tapes, and film documentaries. Teaching same/different concepts should aid in improving verbal abstract reasoning. In addition vocabulary skills can be enhanced by encouraging Michael to learn new words and to read more. Teaching computational skills commensurate with those of his grade peers should aid in improving arithmetic skills. Michael needs the supportive environment of bilingual education and ought to be evaluated bilingually given his reliance on Spanish. Intensive instruction in all academic areas would prove beneficial at this time given the obvious delays in all areas of academia.

This is an educationally and emotionally deprived youngster who was neglected in his native country. Given the fact that emotional factors are impeding his ability to pay attention, to complete class assignments, and to engage his peers socially, intensive management systems are needed in the identified academic and social skills areas. Michael is likely to do better with a lower students-to-teacher ratio and shorter exposure to teaching materials. Overall, Michael will benefit from a highly structured setting and individualized teaching methods.

Summary and Recommendations

Michael is a twelve-year-old who is functioning in the borderline range of intelligence, but who is of low average potential as measured by the Wechsler Intelligence Scale for Children-111. His verbal skills are borderline to low average and his nonverbal skills are low average to average. Visual motor coordination skills are delayed as measured by the Bender test. Academic delays exist in all areas. Emotional factors are impeding learning and affecting peer relations. Michael is self-conscious about his petite bodily frame. Michael is clearly more proficient and dominant in Spanish. Based on the above findings it is recommended that:

1. Michael should receive intensive instruction in all academic skill areas, in particular math, reading, and spelling. Instruction should focus on building English-language skills and vocabulary/communication skills. Given the length of time in this country, his classroom placement should be a nonclassified educational setting.

2. Michael should receive instruction in career awareness and career exploration.

3. Counseling aimed at building self-esteem, self-acceptance, social skills, and communication skills ought to be offered.

4. Family counseling with the goal of improving parent/child communication and teaching the expressing of affection ought to be offered.

5. Michael should be referred to a medical doctor to determine if there are medical difficulties that are causing the headaches and the sleep disturbances.

6. A speech/language evaluation is recommended.

7. Intensive management systems, ranging from teacher-directed to student self-directed, which can lead to improvement in the identified academic and social skill areas ought to be offered.

8. Michael ought to be monitored closely and tested next year to see what progress he is making and if a more or a less restrictive setting would be beneficial.

Tests Administered and Test Results

Wechsler Intelligence Scale for Children-111

Psychometric Assessment		*Range*	
Verbal Scale IQ	70	Borderline	
Performance Scale IQ	79	Borderline	
Full Scale IQ	72	Borderline	

Current Scale Score	*Range*	*Current Scale Score*	*Range*
Information	3	Picture Completion	7
Similarities	2	Coding	6
Arithmetic	7	Picture Arrangement	7
Vocabulary	8	Block Design	7
Comprehension	3	Object Assembly	6
Digit Span	9	Mazes	6

Wechsler Intelligence Scale for Children-111

Psychometric Potential Assessment		*Range*	
Verbal Scale IQ	80	Low average	
Performance Scale IQ	90	Average	
Full Scale IQ	83	Low average	

Potential Scale Score	*Range*	*Potential Scale Score*	*Range*
Information	3	Picture Completion	8
Similarities	5	Coding	6
Arithmetic	9	Picture Arrangement	8
Vocabulary	10	Block Design	9
Comprehension	5	Object Assembly	11
Digit Span	9	Mazes	8

A SECOND BIO-ECOLOGICAL PSYCHOLOGICAL REPORT

Name: Joan   Date of Testing: 1/17/95
School: JHS   Date of Birth: 4/22/84
Grade: 4th   Age: 10 years, 8 months
Language: West Indian Creole

Reason for Referral and Background Information

Joan was referred for an initial evaluation by her teacher due to continued delays in all areas of academia. Joan arrived from Jamaica, West Indies, in March 1994 and entered a New York City school district. In September 1994, she transferred to another school district in New York State. School records from both Jamaica and NYC reveal difficulty in all areas of academia. Teacher reports are very favorable with respect to behavior, motivation, and effort. Currently she is receiving remediation in the core courses. Joan is described as a student who is "noncommunicative in class and does not seem to be aware of what is going on." Although the educational evaluation conducted on 1/11/95 revealed second-grade functioning in math and reading, the classroom teacher's records reflect first-grade functioning in math and reading. According to her teacher, Joan understands much of what is said to her verbally, follows direction well, is "a sweet girl," but lacks basic concepts such as "under," "before," and so on. On the positive side, Joan is said to be a "polite, well mannered girl who tries to relate to her peers even though her social/communicative skills are lacking."

The social history conducted on 12/8/94 revealed that Joan lives with her mother, father, and older brother. The father first came to the United States and left his family in Jamaica. The family including her mother came in March 1994. All developmental milestones were attained at age expectant levels.

Tests Administered and Test Results

Wechsler Intelligence Scale for Children-111

Psychometric Assessment		Range	
Verbal Scale IQ		Moderate retardation	
Performance Scale IQ		Moderate retardation	
Full Scale IQ		Moderate retardation	
Current Scale Score	*Range*	*Current Scale Score*	*Range*
Information	Deficient	Picture Completion	Deficient
Similarities	Deficient	Coding	Borderline
Arithmetic	Borderline	Picture Arrangement	Deficient
Vocabulary	Deficient	Block Design	Deficient

Comprehension	Deficient	Object Assembly	Deficient
Digit Span	Low average	Mazes	—

Psychometric Potential Assessment	Range
Verbal Scale IQ	Borderline
Performance Scale IQ	Borderline
Full Scale IQ	Borderline

Nonpsychometric Ecological Assessment	
Estimated Overall Functioning	Low Average

Other Intelligences Assessment
Bodily Kinesthetic (Volleyball)
Artistic

Family Support Assessment	Moderately low

Bender Gestalt Motor Test	
Koppitz Error Score	9
Age Equivalent	5-9 to 5-11
Bender Recall	1 out of 9

Vineland Behavior Adaptive Scales—Parent Edition	
Communication	Low
Social	Moderately low
Daily Living Scales	Adequate

Social History

Human Figure Drawings

Tell-Me-A-Story (TEMAS)

Clinical Interview

Parent Interview

Teacher Questionnaire

Behavioral Observation

Joan, a pleasant, shy girl, presented herself in a cooperative, compliant manner. In general her response time was slow and she approached the testing in a cautious, reflective manner. When she clearly did not know the answer, she became noticeably frustrated and embarrassed. She would lower her head, frown, and look away from the examiner. Confidence was only noted on the subtest that measures one's ability to recall numbers in a short time frame.

Language Assessment

Joan speaks in both her West Indian dialect as well as in standard English. On this evaluation, she was more dominant socially in West Indian Creole since she tended to respond more spontaneously when she spoke in her native dialect than in English. When asked why she does not speak in the classroom, she stated that "they don't understand me." In spite of having English skills, Joan is too self-conscious to speak in English in the classroom for fear of "saying it wrong." On the Verbal subtest, she repeatedly stated, "I don't know," and only when encouraged was she more responsive.

Psychometric Assessment

On the Wechsler Intelligence Scale for Children-111, Joan obtained a full-scale IQ score which placed her in the very deficient range of intelligence (moderate retardation). Her verbal and nonverbal scores also fell in the moderate range of retardation.

In the verbal area, Joan was very deficient in general information, suggesting that Joan is not yet as alert to the environment and to the social and cultural factors so typical of American society as measured by the WISC-111. Her deficiency in comprehension is also indicative of Joan's limited understanding of the social mores here in the United States at this time as assessed by the Wechsler scales. Joan was also very deficient in verbal abstract reasoning, suggesting that, at this time, Joan has difficulty placing objects and events together in a meaningful group as measured by the WISC-111. In arithmetic and vocabulary, Joan was borderline and deficient respectively. This is indicative of inadequate arithmetic skills as tapped by the WISC-111, as well as poor language development and limited word knowledge. In auditory short-term memory, Joan was low average. Therefore one can expect Joan to be fair at rote memory and sequential processing.

In the nonverbal area, Joan was very deficient in identifying essential missing elements from a whole, suggesting delayed visual alertness, visual discrimination, and long-term visual memory as tapped by the WISC-111. In visual integration, Joan was also deficient, suggesting limited perceptual skills, poor long-term visual memory, and limited constructive ability as measured by the WISC-111. However, Joan was persistent and tried to put the puzzles together. There was a sense that she was unfamiliar with these items. When she was taught how to connect the pieces, she tended to be more relaxed, although she continued to perform poorly. In visual motor coordination/motor speed, Joan was borderline, suggesting slow response time, poor visual short-term memory, and limited visual acuity. Nonverbal comprehension was severely delayed on the WISC-111, suggesting inadequate ability to anticipate the consequences of her actions, to plan, and to organize ahead of time on this type of test. In nonverbal abstract reasoning, Joan was deficient, suggesting delayed ability to perceive, analyze, and synthesize forms on tests such as the Wechsler scales. This also suggests a limited ability to apply logic and reason to spatial relationship problems.

Psychometric Potential Assessment

When Joan was tested to the limits, when she was not placed under time pressure, and when item equivalencies as well as the test-teach-retest techniques were implemented, Joan's score was improved by thirteen IQ points in the verbal area, fourteen IQ points in the nonverbal area, and eleven IQ points in overall intelligence. Thus when Joan was asked to perform skills comparable to the puzzles on the Wechsler scales, she went from deficient to low average. Likewise, when the vocabulary words were contextually determined—that is, Joan was asked to say the words in a surrounding context (and she said, "I migrated to the United States from Jamaica," instead of defining the word "migrate" in isolation), Joan went from deficient to low average. Since vocabulary is the best measure of general intelligence, Joan is at least of borderline potential in the verbal area.

In the nonverbal area, Joan went from deficient to low average on the Block Design subtest when she was taught (test-teach-retest) to manipulate the sample block. Thus again, Joan is of low average potential in the nonverbal area since Block Design is the best measure of nonverbal intelligence on the Wechsler scales. Overall Joan's potential intellectual functioning in the nonverbal area is also borderline.

Nonpsychometric Ecological Assessment

At home and in the community, Joan is described as "industrious and smart" by her family. According to her mother Joan does grocery shopping and cares for the family's basic needs when her mother is at work. Thus she cooks, cleans, irons, and performs all basic household and community chores commensurate with her age peers. Thus in Joan's ecology, that is, in a real-life situation away from the testing environment, she shows good planning ability and good perceptual organization. From an ecological perspective, her intellectual ability is at least low average.

Other Intelligences Assessment

Joan's mother described her as athletic, in particular in volleyball and to a lesser extent in soccer. Her mother said that in the community, Joan is well respected by her peers, who often come to her home to ask her to play various sports. Her gym teacher feels that she has a well-developed sense of timing, coordination, and rhythm when it pertains to playing "all sorts of games and sports." Thus with respect to kinesthetic intelligence, Joan seems to be average in her ability to play volleyball. Likewise, her musical and artistic abilities are described as average by the music and art teachers. This was confirmed by her mother, who stated that Joan is very motivated in the musical and artistic areas.

Visual Motor Assessment

The borderline performance noted in visual motor coordination on the Wechsler scales was also seen on the unstructured Bender test of visual motor coordination. Joan's performance was severely delayed due to nine errors of integration, of rotation, and of distortion. It seems that Joan had difficulties in both the conceptualization of the visual impressions as well as visual perception itself. Thus she not only perceived the Gestalts incorrectly, but also interpreted them in a concrete way to fit her realm of experience at this time. Besides, the designs were executed in a disorganized manner.

Like auditory short-term memory, which was below average, visual memory was deficient since Joan recalled only one of the nine designs. Since Joan did not show a particular strength in either auditory or visual short-term memory, remediation should be undertaken both auditorily as well as visually. Therefore audiotapes as well as computer aids would prove beneficial in remediating Joan in her areas of weakness. Her figure drawings showed timidity and anxiety.

Achievement Testing

The educational evaluation revealed that Joan is on a second-grade level in math and reading. However, Joan's teacher feels that she is on a first-grade level in reading and math, as evidenced by her inability to read and write simple five-word sentences and her inability to perform mathematical computations such as $12 - 5$ or $8 + 8 + 8$. Since she has only been residing in the United States for ten months, it is expected that she would have some adjustment difficulties in the academic or social areas. According to her mother, Joan's school attendance in Jamaica was regular. Thus, Joan would not be considered an educationally deprived student in her native country. It is possible that Joan simply lacks the required skills to best negotiate this environment at the present time. Given her potential, Joan's prognosis for functioning at a higher educational level is fair if she receives intensive instruction in all academic areas.

Personality Assessment

The personality tests, the clinical interview, and the parental interview depict Joan's adjustment as variable. On the one hand she is a pleasant, delightful, motivated, and sensitive youngster. She is interested in learning and wants to be a home care provider, a cook, and a sports person. These positive behaviors are primarily noted at home and in her community. In the school environment, there is a picture of a shy, noncommunicative girl. The personality tests and the teacher interview reveal a girl who is lacking in self-confidence due to continued failure in spite of her avid efforts. What one is also observing is an underlying sense of frustration with respect to limited communication and classroom skills. The result is poor social skills and a lack of involvement in social activities in school. Of note is that Joan's limited socialization is not evident in the community. She is popular, plays sports, and is liked by her peer group in her home community.

Family support is moderately low, although she receives help in her homework. Her mother is a home care provider and her father is a packer for a warehouse. It seems that Joan's parents are willing, but not necessarily able, to assist her as she acclimates to this society. Family counseling should also aid in empowering the family by referring them to community support systems such as a church, or an after-school program. This should help the family in their acculturation process. Individual counseling should also focus on building Joan's self-esteem and her self-confidence. Anxiety reduction training with respect to failing and being "not as smart" should also be provided via counseling.

Diagnostic Impression/Educational Implication

Intellectually Joan is functioning in the moderate range of retardation on the WISC-111 psychometric test. However, given her psychometric potential functioning, she is borderline. Since Joan attended school in her native country on a regular basis, she cannot be said to be educationally deprived. A diagnosis of mental retardation cannot be given either. Although she attained an IQ score of 59 (moderate retardation) on the WISC-111, her potential is at least borderline, and in the case of the Vocabulary and Block Design subtests (the best measures of general intelligence on psychometric tests), Joan was low average. To be classified as mentally retarded, one needs to have concurrent deficits or impairments in at least two areas of adaptive functioning. On the Vineland behavior adaptive scales, Joan was moderately low in social adaptive functioning and was adequate in her ability to carry out daily living skills. It is only on communication skills that she was low, which was commensurate with her score on the WISC-111 psychometric test. Besides, as a family assessment shows, it is clear that Joan functions adequately in her community and is respected by her peers. Thus in spite of communication delays, there are no overall social adaptive deficiencies to characterize her as mentally retarded. At this juncture Joan's intellectual functioning best fits the diagnosis of "learning disabled not otherwise specified." This category is for learning disorders that do not meet the criteria for any specific learning disorder and that may include problems in all three core areas of reading, mathematics, and written expression.

Joan's social and emotional difficulties may be a result of acculturation difficulties. However, given the length of time she has been residing in this country, a diagnosis of adjustment disorder does not seem appropriate. Given her overall social and emotional functioning in the home, school, and community, Joan demonstrates no signs of any personality disorders. Her tendency to be occasionally withdrawn and noncommunicative in the school setting is insufficient to make a diagnosis of emotional disturbance. Her symptoms seem to be more characteristic of a young lady with a poor sense of herself—an overall low self-esteem.

Given Joan's delays in general information, comprehension, vocabulary, arithmetic, and verbal abstract reasoning, remediation should focus on exposure to a broad range of everyday facts, practical reasoning in social situations, and word building. Moreover, teaching same/different concepts should aid in improving verbal abstract reasoning. In addition vocabulary skills can be enhanced by encouraging Joan to learn new words and to read more. Teaching computational skills commensurate with those of her grade peers should aid in improving arithmetic skills. Joan needs the supportive environment of a smaller classroom size where intensive instruction in all academic areas can be offered. Since she has lived for only fourteen months in this country, such a setting should be nonclassified at this time.

Summary and Recommendations

Joan is a ten-year-old girl whose psychometric intelligence is very deficient (moderate retardation) as measured by the Wechsler Intelligence Scale for Children-111. However, Joan is of borderline potential given her potential scores in Vocabulary and Block Design, the best measures of intelligence in the verbal and nonverbal areas respectively. Of note is that she is of low average potential when a more ecological approach to assessment (in keeping with New York state guidelines) was followed. Visual motor coordination skills are delayed as measured by the Bender test. Academic delays exist in all areas. Emotional factors (poor self-esteem and frustration over continued failure) are impeding learning and affecting peer relations at school. However, at home and in her community, Joan is said to engage her peers socially and is liked by them. Joan is more socially comfortable speaking in her native dialect. Based on the above findings it is recommended that:

1. Joan should receive intensive instruction in all academic skill areas, in particular, math, reading, and spelling. Instruction should focus on building vocabulary and communication skills in a nonclassified setting, given the limited time that she has been residing in the United States.

2. Counseling aimed at building self-esteem, self-acceptance, social skills, and communication skills ought to be offered.

3. Family counseling with the goal of empowering the family to use the various programs in the community would prove beneficial. Joan should be encouraged to join social organizations in her community in order to build her social and communication skills.

4. Joan ought to be monitored closely and tested next year to see what progress she is making and if a more or a less restrictive setting would be beneficial. When Joan is tested, modifications should be made such as suspending time on the tests and allowing the use of paper and pencil.

Tests Administered and Test Results

Wechsler Intelligence Scale for Children-111

Psychometric Assessment		Range
Verbal Scale IQ	59	Moderate retardation
Performance Scale IQ	59	Moderate retardation
Full Scale IQ	59	Moderate retardation

Scale Score	Range	Scale Score	Range
Information	3	Picture Completion	1
Similarities	1	Coding	6
Arithmetic	5	Picture Arrangement	1
Vocabulary	4	Block Design	4
Comprehension	1	Object Assembly	4
Digit Span	7	Mazes	—

Wechsler Intelligence Scale for Children-111

Psychometric Potential Assessment		Range	
Verbal Scale IQ	72	Borderline	
Performance Scale IQ	73	Borderline	
Full Scale IQ	70	Borderline	

Scale Score	Range	Scale Score	Range
Information	4	Picture Completion	4
Similarities	3	Coding	6
Arithmetic	8	Picture Arrangement	4
Vocabulary	8	Block Design	7
Comprehension	2	Object Assembly	7
Digit Span	7	Mazes	—

PART III

TREATMENT ISSUES FOR THE CULTURALLY DIFFERENT

7
Issues in Counseling Immigrant Families That Can Affect the Treatment Process

In counseling immigrant families, it is first necessary to examine several cultural issues that may impact on treatment:

1. The concept of mental illness and psychotherapy among immigrants
2. Therapeutic alliance
3. The effects of family role changes and disciplinary practices on acculturation
4. The obligations of children to their parents
5. Language and communication patterns and their impact on acculturation
6. Legal status
7. Ethnicity
8. The race, gender, and culture of the therapist
9. The question of whether the family has acculturated or is in transition

CONCEPT OF MENTAL ILLNESS AND PSYCHOTHERAPY AMONG IMMIGRANTS

Due to a lack of exposure to and familiarity with the field of mental health in their home countries, many immigrants generally do not readily accept psychotherapy. They tend to seek the help of a psychotherapist as a last resort. Another impediment to accepting psychotherapy is the social stigma attached to it. The average person from "lesser developed countries" believes that a person is either normal or "crazy," and only "crazy" people seek psychotherapeutic help. There is little perception of the continuum of behaviors between these two points, nor is there a belief that intervention may prevent things from worsening. For all these reasons, a family may not seek treatment from mental health workers. Only after all internal family measures and the help of ministers and/or spiritists have failed do they enter therapy, feeling ashamed and conquered. The therapist must be sensitive to all of these issues if therapy is to be successful. The therapist can assist the family by demystifying the concept of mental illness, while at the same time respecting this deep-seated cultural belief.

THERAPEUTIC ALLIANCE

In exploring the process in a successful therapeutic alliance, one must begin by examining the client's expectations of the therapist and vice versa. Many people from culturally diverse backgrounds tend to perceive the therapist as an expert, a sort of problem solver who can guide the family in the right direction. The therapist, like the teacher and the medical doctor, is seen as an authority figure and is respected.

However, if the therapist does not fulfill the expectations of the family, he or she may lose their respect, and treatment may be terminated. In general, many families from "third world" countries want a psychotherapist to be active and directive, yet personal, warm, empathetic, and respectful of the family's structure and boundaries. Being active and directive does not mean telling clients what to do or how to live their lives, nor does it mean being too blunt and insensitive; rather, it means taking some initiative and directing the process of the session. For example, the therapist may give some direction as to which family member will speak first; in keeping with the traditional family structure, the husband ought to be addressed first, then the wife, and then the children, according to their ages. If the wife is the one doing most of the talking, the therapist should attempt to assist the husband in commenting on her statements. If he is in agreement with his wife, the therapist can mention this to reinforce their unity. At times, the man's silence may be indicative of his quiet strength and the respect he has for his wife's ability to understand the problems of their children. If he disagrees with her, the therapist can point out the validity of different perspectives and different solutions, while attempting to address the problems.

In most places around the world, people rarely initiate therapy because of marital problems. Those who do so tend to be more acculturated to American society. Most families who seek help do so because of a child's problem for which a medical doctor was unable to find a physiological cause. The alliance with children in therapy depends on their ages. With adolescents, it is important to remember that they may have difficulty speaking in front of their parents, especially their fathers, particularly if the topics discussed include drugs, sex, home conflicts, and school problems. It is important and beneficial to hear the adolescent's concerns in private. It is equally important to convince the parents of the importance of doing this. Many immigrant parents will not automatically respect or even understand this need for confidentiality; for them confidentiality is neither a right nor a given. But if they believe that part of solving the problem involves the acceptance of this process, they will be conciliatory to the therapist's request that they leave the room. Some parents will feel betrayed, however, because, for the most part, they expect the therapist to assume a parental manner. The goal, of course, should be to help the adolescent to express his or her concerns to the parents and to find ways in which children and parents can forge a compromise.

In initiating and maintaining a relationship with a client, it may also help to make home visits, which personalizes the relationship and increases trust. Moreover, in establishing a successful therapeutic alliance, a bit of self-disclosure (but not too much) is helpful, since it gives the family some perspective on the therapist. This does not mean telling one's life story or becoming too casual; but if one is questioned, it may be helpful to reveal enough so the family sees the "human side" of the therapist.

It is important for the family to feel that they can disagree with the therapist. Since immigrants tend to confer much respect on a therapist once trust has been established, it is difficult for them to express anger or criticism toward the therapist, especially if the therapist has been helpful in resolving some family conflicts because obligation was thus incurred. The therapist must be responsive to nonverbal cues, such as changes in facial expression, sudden silence, or changes in vocal inflection, all of which may be indirect indicators that someone is angry or not in agreement and is trying to suppress his or her feelings. Such suppression of feelings is also noted among lower-status individuals toward higher-status individuals in the family. It is likely that this reluctance to open up may result in the family's terminating treatment without even telling the therapist why.

In general, in order to establish a successful therapeutic alliance, it is necessary to explore the cultural strengths of the family, demonstrate a caring attitude, and be directive, warm, and "human," but not too friendly. In addition, it is best to be flexible with respect to home visits.

In spite of all attempts to foster a therapeutic alliance, many immigrant families remain resistant to therapy. Two factors in particular impact on resistance with the immigrant family: the concepts of time and family secrets. Lack of observance of scheduled appointment times is a major concern in therapy with immigrant families, who do not have the same concept of time as North Americans tend to. In fact, in many cultures, people endorse the adage "better late than never." Besides, in many cultures, people tend to visit friends to socialize at any time without having received an invitation or without calling. Because of the informality of their homelands, many clients miss appointments or appear at unscheduled times, expecting to be seen. It is important for the therapist to explain the process of treatment and that timeliness is important since they will have less therapy time for the same money that they are spending. This will be quite effective, since in spite of their tardiness, immigrants give priority to job demands and will not sacrifice work for therapy, because they take very seriously the aphorism "time is money." However, such behavior does not necessarily reflect resistance to therapy. A therapist may therefore have to be flexible in scheduling treatment, so that therapy does not interfere with educational or work opportunities. If treatment results in the loss of money, the family or individual may become resistant and resentful.

While immigrants may even come to psychotherapy, sharing real family secrets is a different issue. Secrets are to be kept within the family unit. Every child is told very early, "Do not put our business on the street." Therefore, openly and freely discussing personal and family issues with a stranger is often very difficult. Many immigrant families also tend to deny family problems because they believe there is nothing that they cannot solve from within the family. They indulge in much circumlocution, especially in the initial stages of therapy. Thus, unless the therapist has clinical evidence that maintaining secrets is hindering the therapeutic process, the therapist is advised particularly in the initial stages to proceed on the assumption that keeping secrets may merely be a maneuver to keep boundaries in place. Pushing the family to tell their secrets too early in therapy may provoke mistrust and resistance, thus jeopardizing the therapist's position.

In general, immigrant families see the therapists as an expert or a teacher who is supposed to solve the problem quickly. Thus the short-term behavioral therapy is more effective with immigrant clients. In general, therapists are viewed as authority figures and are expected to play a significantly active role in the lives of their clients. They are seen as powerful, a sort of scholar, but are still expected to respect the cultural boundaries as they address the client's needs.

THE EFFECTS OF FAMILY ROLE CHANGES AND DISCIPLINARY PRACTICES ON ACCULTURATION

In traditional cultures, interpersonal relations and interactions are determined primarily by expected roles, duties, and obligations. The role structure is hierarchical and vertical, determined by age and gender. Even if a woman is a professional, her role is primarily one of childrearing and caring for the emotional well-being of her family. Therefore, if a child is having psychological problems, the woman is held accountable. Her most important bond is with her children rather than her husband.

In most patriarchal cultures, the father is the financial provider and the disciplinarian when the mother "cannot handle the children." His strongest bond is usually with his mother rather than his wife. Due to the unequal power distribution between parents and children, there is always a need for an intermediary, who may be a well-respected aunt or uncle or even a "parental" child. The "parental" child is usually the caretaker for the younger ones when the parents are not at home.

The oldest son has many roles. He has to be an emotional support to his mother, and he is often an intermediary between his parents, since should the situation arise, he is expected to defend his mother against his father's abuses. He is also responsible for his younger siblings' educational development and is a financial contributor to his family.

The youngest child may, as an adult, be expected to stay at home with the parents. Since this child is the one likely to be the most acculturated to American ways, having migrated at the youngest age, he or she tends to be most vulnerable to familial conflicts due to cultural differences.

Changes in family roles markedly affect acculturation. Since many cultures are patriarchal in nature, migration to the United States results in a loss of power for the males. A man may lose his power in decision making and may no longer be the family's sole breadwinner, possibly resulting in a loss of self-esteem. Sharing power with his wife (a discrepancy between U.S. cultural attitudes and those of many cultures) may make the man feel disrespected and as if he is a failure as a man. The man experiences greater displacement if he is unable to obtain employment, while his wife can, and he has to remain at home to care for the children. This shift in marital roles may not be as distressing for the man if the woman maintains a traditional perspective on family life. Usually, however, the wife feels more independent and becomes more assertive. If the wife becomes too assertive and challenges his authority and reminds him who is bringing in the money, the husband may then feel emasculated; often this results in depression. If the man is unable to regain his position of dominance through the major means he was taught—employment—he can panic and attempt to assert his authority in an abusive manner. The end result may be separation due to marital discord, caused by the feelings of helplessness and confusion about role change.

Likewise, women no longer totally value domestic life as their center and are no longer defined mainly by their roles as wives and mothers, but are also employed outside the home. Some even return to school and therefore advance themselves educationally and professionally.

Children also go through periods of role change. They observe their American counterparts and are impressed with their assertiveness and independence. The children come to resent their parents' rigid controls, imposed structure, and authoritarian behaviors. They become angry and frustrated about their parents' traditional and "outdated" modes of disciplining them and solving family problems. For example, in an anecdote that highlights the high regard and respect some immigrant families have for teachers, one parent was so appalled at her son's defiance of a teacher that she scolded and spanked him in the presence of his teacher, actually taking the child's pants down to spank him on the buttocks. The teacher was amazed at such "autocratic measures," claiming "this was a bit abusive." But this is not atypical among many cultural groups, even though more acculturated and assimilated immigrant families, who are more familiar with the American social, legal, and political systems, usually do not resort to such measures.

Payne (1989) administered a questionnaire to 499 Barbadians, excluding teachers and child-care workers, to determine their views on corporal punishment. This study found that corporal punishment was seen as a means of "teaching right from wrong, lessening the risks of law-breaking when older, training children to grow up in a respectable and decent manner" (p. 397). Payne (1989) also found that the majority (76.5%) endorsed flogging or lashing with a belt or strap as an approved method, with the buttocks most frequently identified as the part of the anatomy to which it should be administered. Slapping with the hand, spanking with a shoe, and hitting the knuckles or palm of the hand with a ruler were approved by 14.4 percent, 14.2 percent, and 5.4 percent respectively. Burning and scalding (traditional methods used to punish stealing) and lashing out at the child with any object at hand were the forms of corporal punishment most strongly disapproved of. Payne (1989) also noted the types of misconduct for which corporal punishment was considered most appropriate—disrespect to parents and elders, dishonesty, disobedience, stealing, indecent language, violence, deliberate defiance, disregarding the rules of the home or the community, and laziness and neglect of chores. Although this study was conducted only in Barbados, West Indies, the biblical maxim "To spare the rod is to spoil the child" is the general sentiment shared by most cultures around the world. Therefore, mental health practitioners and researchers need to adopt a cross-cultural, dual perspective in conceptualizing and defining child abuse, neglect, and maltreatment among immigrant families. The tasks of the therapist, therefore, are to educate the parents to alternative ways of disciplining their children and to help mitigate the guilt, shame, and cultural conflict that the children experience when they are spanked or reprimanded in the presence of their peers or teachers. Therapists must pay close attention to all these factors and familial roles, since these issues are all played out in therapy.

THE OBLIGATIONS OF CHILDREN TO THEIR PARENTS

American culture emphasizes self-reliance and independence with high value being placed on one's ability to pull one's self up by one's bootstraps without relying on others. In contrast, many people from varying cultural backgrounds believe that a person is what he or she is due to the support of, and his or her relationship with, many people, especially family members. Therefore, the concept of obligation and reciprocity is crucial and is a dictum that everyone understands. This obligation is born of ascribed roles and the understanding of the hierarchical nature of the relationship, such as parent/child, employer/employee, or teacher/pupil. This obligatory reciprocity also derives from the sacrifices made by individuals. Many immigrant families are known to work as many as three jobs if that is necessary to give their children an education. One woman illustrated the general attitude when she said, "If I have to be a slave in someone's kitchen, I will do it for my son to be a doctor. I do not think about it. I just do it." In the face of that kind of unflagging support, the greatest obligation children feel is toward their parents. Children feel they can never really repay such a debt, so they give respect to their parents at all costs, even if it means interrupting their own personal lives. It is important for a therapist to understand this obligation, because much difficulty may arise if a therapist tries to help an individual separate or individuate from his or her family. Giving adolescents assertiveness training without understanding this family ethic can be more problematic than beneficial. Thus it may be more helpful to solicit the help of a significant and close family member, such as an uncle, aunt, or grandparent, who can convey to the parents what the child is experiencing. In other words, detriangulating the most significant people who can aid in the assimilation process would start the ripple effect of change throughout the rest of the family system.

Another area of concern is that children are expected to maintain loyalties to their parents' cultural values. Many parents expect their children to remain enmeshed with the family, because they are concerned that the children will get

Americanized and "get lost in the system." The family therefore closes its boundaries to the outside world, participating in few cultural events and using few support facilities. This fear of the new environment and a longing for the old one cause the family to isolate itself from the new environment. In attempting to cope, the child may disengage from the family and reject its values. The problem here is that both the child and the family may become vulnerable to an environment that neither knows how to fully negotiate. Children who are caught between conflicts of cultures may develop a negative sense of self and a poor self-image. The therapist needs to assist youngsters in integrating old values with newly learned ones, in respecting the values of the older generation while forging on and forming their own. An important factor is the sensitivity of the therapist to the preservation of continuities during this fragile process of change. To expect an individual, especially an adult, to become completely Americanized can create anxiety and a feeling of a loss of control. It may be beneficial to teach the adolescents to select the best of both cultures and incorporate those values into their pool of coping skills.

LANGUAGE AND COMMUNICATION PATTERNS AND THEIR IMPACT ON ACCULTURATION

When clients find themselves having to repeat their answers because of the difficulty the therapist has in understanding them, they tend to become very frustrated and feel that the therapist will not be able to assist them. In other words, they equate the understanding of their language with the understanding of their culture. Some families who are already skeptical about the treatment process use this as an opportunity to terminate therapy. Of course, the potential cultural barriers are reduced if the therapist can understand the language or dialect and the nonverbal language. The therapist ought to tune in to the client's use of cultural proverbs and nonverbal body language, such as eye contact. Direct eye contact on a continuous basis can be perceived as threatening; in the case of an opposite-sex therapist/client relationship (especially if the therapist is a woman), it may even be perceived as a sexual overture. When the individual feels at liberty to express himself or herself, rapport may be established more easily and the possibility of a positive outcome may increase. Moreover, the therapist must be sensitive to topics that the client has difficulty discussing. For instance, discussing sexual matters creates discomfort, especially in older women. Talking about impending death is considered ominous and may be thought to be a sign of bad luck. Such matters should be broached only after a therapeutic alliance has been established.

LEGAL STATUS

To a large extent the legal status of clients or of school children determines whether they will feel comfortable opening up to a therapist. Therapists ought to familiarize themselves with the immigration laws (Gopaul-McNicol, 1993) to best service these families.

ETHNICITY

Racism presents serious problems for many immigrant families while acculturating. To begin with, many immigrants in their native lands were not in the minority because of the existing homogeneous societies around the world. Therefore, African Americans and many immigrants have difficulty endorsing such labels as "minority," "disadvantaged," and "oppressed."

THE RACE, GENDER, AND CULTURE OF THE THERAPIST

Since most cultures are patriarchal, vertical, and hierarchical in their family structure, many immigrants who come into therapy "tend to respond best to an older male therapist because this is syntonic with the cultural respect most feel for men and elders" (Brice, 1982, p. 130). Therefore, in working with immigrant families, an inexperienced therapist, especially one who is female or young, may do well to solicit the support of a co-therapist who fits this image or of extended family elders who can serve as intermediaries between the therapist and the family. The latter course of action would show that the therapist recognizes and respects the value of elders in the family and society. Male/female team therapy is recommended in such a case. A caveat here is that, while clients may more readily take directives from a male, they may speak more easily to a woman about emotional matters, since women tend to handle such issues in the family. However, both men and women will respect a therapist whom they perceive as a knowledgeable expert.

A therapist of a different culture may encounter difficulties in working with some immigrant families. A therapist needs to begin by exploring his or her stereotypes, attitudes, and feelings about the culture in question. In general, a degree of cultural understanding and similarity helps. A therapist who has experience with immigrant families in general has a greater chance of success in working with clients from diverse cultural backgrounds. However, such a therapist must be careful of making generalizations and assuming that all immigrants will respond in a similar manner to a particular problem. Likewise, the therapist ought not to assume that a client of a different race from that of the therapist will have problems identifying with the therapist. Carter (1995) outlines issues of race in psychotherapy, and Chapter 11 also attempts to capture some of the salient issues raised by authors who believe a race inclusive model should be included in psychotherapy (Carter, 1995). A caveat, though, is that some culturally diverse clients of African ancestry have not conceptualized racism in the manner that African Americans here in the United States have. This may be because in their native lands, there were no impassable barriers between the races which were upheld by institutional racism as is seen here in the United States. By contrast "the brutality of racism was softened and masked by the concept of social color" (Gopaul-McNicol, 1993, p. 52). Thus a person's particular classification was determined more by his/her education, social position, and wealth, and not as much by his/her skin color. As a result, a therapist has to be careful that he/she does not make any assumptions about a client's feelings about him/her because he/she is of a different race.

THE QUESTION OF WHETHER A FAMILY HAS ACCULTURATED OR IS IN TRANSITION

Individuals who immigrate experience several stages of cultural transition. The first is a physical transition requiring economic security, employment and educational opportunities, and the ability to communicate in the host country and to understand the social and political differences between it and one's native land. The second is cognitive and affective in nature. In this stage the family has to deal with the psychological pain of "letting go" and assimilating to the new country. In other words, physically arriving in the United States does not necessarily mean that one has emotionally arrived. It is like a person who wants a divorce, but is nevertheless pained by the severing of ties with his or her spouse. This is the most difficult stage. The loss of family, friends, and culture, along with the change in family roles, the hope of "returning home one day," the state of uncertainty, and the expectation that one has to adapt and acculturate immediately can lead to stress and dysfunction. Some possible cognitive and affective responses or reactions are

- Grief at the loss of culture, family, friends, and so forth
- Culture shock and disappointment at the discrepancy between expectation and reality
- Frustration, anger, and resentment
- Depression
- Acceptance

Gopaul-McNicol (1993) outlines several factors that may influence the differences in the rates of acculturation among individuals:

- Whether they are first-, second-, or third-generation Americans. The longer a family is in the United States, the easier the acculturation process tends to become. However, the number of years in the United States is not the absolute measure, since many immigrants attempt to preserve their culture by freezing traditions.
- Whether they are children of mixed (intercultural) marriages. This can ease the process of acculturation, since one parent is familiar with the workings of American culture.
- Their language. Fluency in English aids in the assimilation process.
- Their immigration status. Being in the United States legally makes for greater stability and more opportunities for scholarships and higher-paying jobs.
- Their educational and professional backgrounds. Professional affiliations tend to open doors and help accelerate the acculturation process. Resources such as status and money increase their esteem among Americans.
- Their age at the time of migration. The younger the individual, the easier the assimilation process should be.

One's ability to acculturate is a crucial indicator of one's willingness to change familial roles—a much needed aspect in cultural assimilation. Of particular importance is the fact that in most cases, migrants are separated from their families for more years than was anticipated, because of the length of time it takes for them to become eligible to sponsor their families. Contact is maintained by mail and telephone, and migrants usually send goods and money home to their families regularly. Spouses tend to join the immigrants first, followed by the children. Often the children come at different times, depending on the immigrants' financial stability. Most immigrants continue to work more than one job in order to bring up members of their extended families. Thus it is not unusual for an immigrant family to be comprised of the nuclear family, grandparents, aunts, uncles, godparents, and even friends. In a sense, this family structure is akin to a multigenerational type of household, with everyone playing a role in disciplining and caring for the children. Thus when gathering information on a client, one may have to be patient if the biological parents are not forthcoming with all of the family background. Because of the prolonged separation of children from their parents, the parents may not be cognizant of many important stages in the child's development. The parents may not be aware of information such as medical inoculation, diseases, and other developmental milestones. Some therapists mistakenly view these parents as "uncaring" because they are ignorant of such important information. It is important, therefore, that when a therapist is developing social services for such families, they do not do so from the perspective of the traditional nuclear family, a constellation of biological parents and their children. Due to the prolonged separation, children may not view the parents as the primary caretakers and may continue to seek the guidance of their grandparents or significant others. The parent who so desperately wants to be the primary parent figure again may resent this, and parent/child conflict may result.

Some of the conflicts center around cultural differences in disciplining, parents' unfamiliarity with age-appropriate behaviors for typical American children who are their children's counterparts, and parental unavailability to the children and to school personnel because they have several jobs. It is important to remember that a major aspect of a family in transition is its need for financial security about the fundamental necessities of life—food, shelter, clothing, and so on. The reestablishing of the parent's role as the primary authority figure and the transition from one culture to the next are difficult processes, particularly since grandparents or other extended family members often intervene unconsciously in defense of the children. In addition, parents may feel that the many sacrifices they made and abuses they endured to create a better life for their children are not appreciated. These issues, coupled with such changes as those in school, peers, environment, weather, and political climate, all exacerbate the tension for the culturally different family.

8
Current Major Approaches in Counseling Culturally Different Families

With the continued increase of immigrants entering the United States from various cultures, researchers, teachers, and mental health workers are faced with the challenge of acquiring a working knowledge of each group's customs, norms, history, and so forth. While it is impossible for any therapist to understand the traditions, values, and languages of all immigrant groups, a therapist (in spite of his or her limited knowledge) may be guided by a conceptual, operational principle that can be implemented across diverse groups and circumstances. This chapter explores several treatment techniques that can apply to immigrants, with particular attention to the works of Sue (1981), Pedersen (1985), Helms (1985), Dillard (1983) (emphasis on culture—multicultural); Lazarus (1976), Bowen (1978), Minuchin (1974) (different modes of therapy—multimodal, educational, structural); and Boyd-Franklin (1989) (multisystems).

MULTICULTURAL COUNSELING

Multicultural counseling has become a popular concept among practitioners and researchers because it is a way to acknowledge cultural diversity between therapist and client. Dillard (1983) includes in the definition of *culture* a shared belief system, behavioral styles, symbols, and attitudes within a social group. Assimilating to a particular culture is a slow process that involves the stage of acculturation, that is, adopting some dominant social and cultural norms and possibly losing a sense of cultural identity with one's original culture. In attempting to conduct multicultural counseling, the goal must be to assist the culturally different client to adapt to or reshape his or her psychosocial environment (Dillard, 1983). Sue (1981) examined the underlying principles in attempting to counsel the culturally different. His major point was the importance of the therapist's being knowledgeable about the client's culture and lifestyle in order to provide culturally responsive forms of treatment. Sue and Zane (1987) emphasized that changes had to do with the process of "match or fit." Treatment should match or fit the cultural lifestyles or experiences of clients in order to prevent premature termination and underutilization of services and ultimately to result in positive outcomes. Thus knowledge of the culture, the formulation of culturally relevant and consistent strategies, credibility (the client's perception of the therapist as an effective and trustworthy helper), and giving (the client's perception that something was received from the therapeutic encounter) are all necessary in providing more adequate service to the culturally different.

Implicit in cross-cultural psychology is the notion of biculturalism. Many theorists view biculturalism as the healthiest identity resolution in the United States, although some view it as an abandonment of one's cultural heritage. Pedersen (1985) sees biculturalism as an addition to one's original heritage and examines the process by which cultural identity develops, since intercultural interactions influence one's behavior. Helms (1985) outlines the three stages of cultural identity.

Stage one, the preencounter stage, is the phase before the individual's cultural awakening. In this stage, the individual is so enmeshed in the Eurocentric view that he or she idealizes White culture while degrading his or her own culture of origin. The affective state associated with stage one is poor individual and group self-esteem.

Stage two, the transitional phase, occurs when the individual comes to realize his or her lack of absolute acceptance by the White world. The individual goes through a period of withdrawal and cultural reassessment, ultimately deciding to become a member of his or her own cultural group. Dillard (1983) points out that in this stage the individual sees his or her cultural systems as superior to other cultural systems. It is a stage of ethnocentrism. The affective state is one of euphoria, a sort of spiritual rebirth, as the individual tries to identify with his or her culture of origin. However, there is also confusion and sadness as the individual realizes that there has been some loss of cultural identity since he or she cannot identify with all the values of the original culture.

The final or transcendent stage occurs when the person becomes bicultural and uses the experiences from both cultural groups to best fit his or her own circumstances. In this stage, the individual is more accepting of the flaws in both cultures and does not idealize either group. Affect is less tempered, and an identity resolution is experienced. Interpersonal relations are not limited by race, culture, gender, and so forth; a broader perspective is endorsed. Self-esteem is improved. This stage is attained after one experiences an identity transformation, via personal readiness and educational and cultural-socialization experiences requiring cultural flexibility. Recommendations for therapists on how to best treat individuals in these various stages are discussed in Chapter 9.

MULTIMODAL THERAPY

The aim of multimodal therapy is to reduce psychological discomfort and promote individual growth by recognizing that few, if any, problems have a single cause or a single cure. Instead, the disquietude of people is multilayered, requiring a holistic understanding of one's interactions. Lazarus (1976) dissected human personality by examining the interaction among multiple modalities—behavior, affect, sensations, images, cognitions, interpersonal, and biological (BASIC IB). To make the acronym more compelling—BASIC ID—the biological modality was called "D" for "drugs," although it actually includes the full range of medical interventions (e.g., nutrition, hygiene, exercise, medication). The multimodal assessment focuses on the behaviors that are getting in the way of one's happiness and how one behaves when he or she feels (affect) a certain way, as well as what the sensations (e.g., aches and pains) are and what bearings these sensations have on behavior and feelings. In addition, the goal is to examine how one perceives one's body and self-image, how one's cognitions affect one's emotions, and what one's intellectual interests are. Who the most important people in one's life (interpersonal) are and what they are doing to one are also explored. Moreover, the focus is on any concerns one has about the state of one's health and the drugs or medication that one uses.

Educational Approach

Bowen's (1978) systems therapy, in which the therapist is portrayed as a teacher who utilizes an educational approach to therapy, is quite compatible with the perspective of many culturally diverse people's manner of securing and accepting help. This approach recognizes the value of education and research toward self-change. Bowen, also an advocate of the multigenerational perspective, focuses on transgenerational patterns. Thus, what has occurred in the past and what the older generation feels about it are important in Bowenian therapy. One goal of therapy is to increase differentiation of individuals within their families. Another goal is to decrease individual anxiety and emotional reactivity by diverting the focus from the "identified patient" to past and present family members. If this is done, the individual is allowed to think clearly and avoid the need for triangulation or emotional cutoff, which Bowen believes occurs when anxiety is high. He more often engages in couple therapy than in family therapy, but he encourages couples to work on their relationships with their families of origin, based on the assumption that unresolved issues with one's original family affect current family relations. Therapy constitutes a cognitive reencounter with one's past as it is represented in one's present life. The focus is on facts and patterns, not feelings. He also establishes a leverage within the family system by discovering the most likely entry point (the person most capable of change, that is, the least resistant family member). He then uses this least resistant, most motivated member to deal with the resistance of other family members. His concept of the "coach" is very applicable in working with immigrant families. Rather than meeting with the family, Bowen has the person who came to therapy coach other family members into emotionally mature relationships with one another. This "coaching" approach has been found to be very helpful (Gopaul-McNicol, 1993), because it is very difficult to get an entire family to come into therapy. Since the men are so resistant and tend to deny the therapist adequate entry, using a coach may be the next most effective approach. In addition, the term "family therapy" can be quite threatening to immigrant families who may surmise that the entire family is being seen as dysfunctional. Bowen's "coaching," which makes it unnecessary for the entire family to be present simultaneously, is also useful because immigrant parents often have difficulty engaging in discussions in the presence of their children, which is the typical mode of family therapy. Through this technique, members who may not have otherwise become involved in therapy may be treated. Gopaul-McNicol (1993) has found that the best coach is the eldest male child. While the mother is traditionally the intermediary between the father and the children, in the final analysis, she is expected to side with the father, especially in the presence of the children. The eldest son, by virtue of being a male and an elder offspring, is the one who can gain the respect of the younger siblings (because he himself is still in cultural transition), as well as get the attention of his parents, especially his father, because of his seniority in the hierarchical family structure.

Structural Approach

The structural approach to family therapy is mainly associated with Minuchin (1974). The focus is mainly on boundaries, the patterns of the family, and the relationship between the family system and its wider ecological environment. An individual's symptoms are perceived as due to a family's failure to accommodate its structure to the changing developmental and environmental requirements. These dysfunctional reactions to stress create problems that manifest themselves in family interrelations. The responsibility for change rests primarily on the therapist, who utilizes three strategies—challenging the symptom, the family structure, and the family reality. The therapist has to negotiate the family boundary in such a manner as to be given the power to be therapeutic. These boundary issues incorporate the concepts of enmeshment (some or all of the family members are relatively undifferentiated or permeable) and disengagement (family members behave in a nonchalant manner, since they have little to do with one another, because family boundaries are very rigid and impermeable).

While most families fall within the normal range, Boyd-Franklin (1989) stated that the cultural norm among Black families tends to fall within the enmeshed range. Aponte (1976), one of Minuchin's colleagues, discusses the issue of the power of some family members, who may or may not be in therapy with the identified patient. Aponte emphasizes that even if one conducts several therapy sessions with the identified patient and other family members, change may be sabotaged because of a powerful family member who did not become involved in the therapeutic process. These powerful members may influence the other members to terminate or continue treatment. Thus the therapist is advised to explore as early as possible who the truly powerful family members are. The therapists need to find out such information as whom the client goes to before making a decision, which family member has the final say on most matters (in most societies around the world, it tends to be the father), whom the client listens to most in the family, and who tends to disagree most with the client's decision. These questions can help in identifying the powerful figure who needs to be more directly involved in therapy.

MULTISYSTEMS APPROACH

Boyd-Franklin (1989) emphasized that effective therapy with Black families requires from the therapist a flexibility that allows her or him to draw from different systems theories and incorporate them into an overall treatment plan. It also requires the therapist to intervene at a variety of systems levels, such as individual, family, extended family, church, community, and social services. Boyd-Franklin's multisystems approach has been quite challenging to traditional theories in the field of mental health. Many clinicians feel that working with social service agencies and churches is the task of a social worker and not a clinician. Many therapists feel overwhelmed by the complexity of this multisystems model.

However, in working with Black families, establishing rapport and building credibility are necessary and may involve intervening in numerous systems and at many levels. This model was built on work done by Minuchin et al. (1967), Minuchin's (1974) structural family systems model, Aponte's (1976) ecostructural approach, work by Aponte and Van Deusen (1981), and the ecological approach of a number of theorists, such as Auerswald (1968), Bronfenbrenner (1977), Falicov (1988), Hartman (1978), and Hartman and Laird (1983).

The multisystems approach, which comprises two main axes, is based on a concept of circularity rather than linearity, as are most treatment approaches. Axis I, the treatment process, is composed of the basic components of the therapeutic process: joining, engaging, assessing, problem solving, and interventions designed to restructure and change family systems. Each component can recur throughout the treatment process at all systems levels. Axis II, the multisystems levels, is made up of levels at which the therapist can provide treatment, such as individual, family, extended family, nonblood kin and friends, church, community, social service agencies, and other outside systems.

THE INTEGRATION OF THE THREE APPROACHES

The three approaches—multicultural, multimodal, and multisystems—can be effectively combined in a treatment process in working with immigrant families. In my clinical experience with culturally diverse families, I have found that it is necessary to gain knowledge of the various cultures that impact on a child within his or her family system. Knowledge of a client's culture should help the counselor know how and when to intervene to promote healthy development.

The multimodal approach, which emphasizes therapeutic pluralism, utilizes a multilayered approach to address human discomfort. The goal is to assess the individual through several modalities and then examine the salient interactions among them. Via this approach, a therapist is able to achieve a thorough understanding of the individual and his or her social environment.

Bowen's educational approach helps in clarifying the power within the family and the process of multigenerational interactions. The focus is on facts and patterns of behavior rather than on feelings. This approach can be quite helpful, since in the initial stages of therapy many culturally diverse families can be quite unrevealing of their feelings.

The structural approach helps in restructuring the family that may be too enmeshed or disengaged. This approach is helpful with immigrant families who find themselves losing many of their boundaries during the process of acculturation.

The multisystems approach is useful with immigrant families whose experiences traditionally extend to support systems outside of the nuclear family—the extended family, nonblood kin and friends, and churches. Although the educational and legal systems were barely examined in Boyd-Franklin's multisystems model, they were discussed in great detail in Gopaul-McNicol (1993), since these two systems tend to be very significant as a point of intervention with culturally different families. In particular, the legal institution, specifically with respect to immigration status, constitutes an important systems level.

In summary, treating immigrant families requires the use of multisystems, knowledge of the culture of the family one is treating, and the understanding of how psychopathology is experienced and manifested. It is necessary to respect the family's belief in their cultural religious folk practices. Clearly a review of the international literature on family therapy reveals how culture influences, defines, and shapes the family structure, family practices, family responsibilities, and roles. Likewise, culture determines how people conceptualize psychotherapy. Moreover, it is critical that the therapist be familiar with his or her own culture and their own cultural beliefs.

9

A Multicultural /Multimodal /Multisystems Approach to Working with Immigrant Families: A New Paradigm

In general, treatment with immigrant families can be best understood via a comprehensive model—the Multicultural/Multimodal/Multisystems (MULTI-CMS) approach proposed by Gopaul-McNicol (1993). She emphasized that effective therapy with immigrant families requires from the therapist a flexibility that allows him or her to draw from different systems theories and incorporate them into an overall treatment plan. It requires the therapist to intervene at various levels—individual, family, extended family, church, community, and social services. This approach has been found to be most effective with immigrant families because it provides a flexible set of guidelines for intervention. This approach also recognizes that within the community, the idea that "it takes a whole community to raise a child" is fully endorsed by most people. Thus empowering them to use all of the support systems available to them is crucial to the treatment process. The use of these systems can be implemented at any stage in therapy, but the families must be aware of all potential systems before therapy is terminated so that they can readily tap into them if the need arises. Encouraging the individual to embrace the support of his or her extended family and nonblood kin and of churches in areas such as child care and education may help in preventing personal difficulties.

Unlike many treatment approaches, which are based on linear models, the MULTI-CMS approach is based on the concept of circularity and is composed of four phases. Therefore, each component of each phase can recur repeatedly at various levels throughout treatment. The therapist must therefore be willing and flexible to intervene at whichever phase and whatever level in therapy. With this understanding, the flow of treatment for the multicultural/multimodal/multisystems approach is as follows:

Phase I. Assessment process

    Step 1. Initial assessment

        A. Explaining the process

        B. Establishing trust

    Step 2. Gathering information

    Step 3. Determining the stage of acculturation

    Step 4. Outlining the goals

Phase II. Educational treatment process

Phase III. Psychological treatment process

Phase IV. Empowerment treatment process

PHASE I: ASSESSMENT PROCESS

Step 1: Initial Assessment

The initial assessment stage, which occurs in the first therapy session, is broken into two phases: (1) explaining the process and (2) establishing trust. Because therapy is a relatively new phenomenon among many immigrants from "third world" countries, and because most immigrants are taught to heal themselves within their own familial context, initially most immigrants are resistant to therapy. Thus when immigrant families enter into treatment, it is generally because they were referred by school personnel or child protective services due to difficulty with their children in school or due to charges of child abuse or inappropriate ways of disciplining their children. In an effort to establish a relationship, the therapist must explain the therapeutic process as clearly as possible because many immigrants view psychotherapy as a visit to a medical doctor. Many do not understand how merely talking about one's problem can bring about relief and an actual change. Many believe that therapy will be for only one session and that only the identified patient (in most cases, a child) will be involved. Most families, especially those referred by child protective services, do not believe they should be there; as far as they are concerned, their forms of discipline are appropriate. To the therapist this attitude may appear resistant, but from the clients' perspective, it is sensible. This is because in most of their countries of origin, corporal punishment is an acceptable form of discipline. Therefore it is important that the therapist not degrade the disciplinary measures they have used in the past, but rather explain alternative ways to corporal punishment. It is also necessary to explain that a therapist works with "normal, healthy" people who are simply experiencing adjustment difficulties, not just "crazy" people, as they tend to believe. The therapist should explain that therapy usually lasts approximately one hour and at times it may be necessary to see the entire family, not only the identified patient. Thus, the first few minutes of therapy involves clearing up the misconceptions about psychotherapy and explaining the process of treatment.

Questions can include the following:

1. Why are you here? Given their response, help alleviate any guilt or anger via empathetic understanding. If their understanding of why they are there is different from that of the referral source, the therapist should mention the discrepancy only if it will not hurt the therapeutic alliance. If there is denial on the clients' part, it can be addressed later in the session.
2. Were you ever in therapy before? If they were not, explain the therapeutic process.
3. What are your thoughts about a psychotherapist or about psychotherapy? Address their misconceptions or anger about being in therapy.
4. What do you think you can gain from therapy? In other words, what does the client want the therapist to address immediately? Addressing what the family views as most pressing will help to build the therapist's credibility as well as empower the family.

It might also be important to note the following:

1. The seating arrangement of family members—who sits next to whom?
2. Who is the powerful figure in the family?
3. Who speaks on behalf of the family?
4. Are the children allowed to speak?
5. What significant family members are missing?

The next stage of this initial assessment process is the establishment of trust. This can be done through Sue's concepts of credibility and giving. Credibility, according to Sue and Zane (1987), refers to the client's perception of the therapist as an effective and trustworthy helper. Credibility can be ascribed or achieved. Giving is the client's perception that something was gained from the therapeutic encounter. For most culturally diverse families, a therapist is more credible based on his or her ascribed status in keeping with cultural factors: age, gender, and education. In most societies around the world, the youth is subordinate to the elder, the female to the male, and the less educated individual to the more educated authority figure. A lack of ascribed credibility may be the main reason clients from such societies resist therapy.

Credibility can also be achieved (instead of ascribed) based on the therapist's culturally relevant techniques, skills, and empathetic understanding. A lack of achieved credibility may be the reason clients terminate therapy prematurely. This is why the first session is so important in establishing credibility. Generally clients will trust and view the therapist as more credible if he or she conceptualizes the problem in a manner consistent with their cultural experiences and beliefs. Thus it may be more beneficial, for example, if the therapist appears understanding (not necessarily supportive) as to how a parent can spank a child. Conversely, a therapist who tells a child to be very assertive to his or her parents may lose credibility.

It is important to remember that with this model, the assessment process (as is the therapeutic process) is ongoing and cyclic. Another important factor is that from the inception of therapy, the therapist is engaging in some form of intervention, some sort of problem solving, since the client's fears, misconceptions, and confusion are being alleviated within minutes of the first session.

Step 2: Gathering Information

Therapists need to be aware that with most immigrants, copious note taking can be quite intimidating and distracting, since families may feel the therapist is not paying attention. Thus it is advised that note taking be kept to a minimum and the establishment of trust be the focus in the initial stage of treatment. The genogram, a tool derived from anthropology but quite commonly used in psychology, is a sort of family tree. This can prove to be quite useful to the therapist working with culturally diverse families because of the many family members and friends who are directly or indirectly involved. If nothing else, it will allow the individual or family to visually represent their support systems. It can be equally beneficial simply to record the information without the use of a tree using such questions as Who raised you? Whom did you live with prior to coming to the United States? Once a picture has been drawn, the therapist can encourage the family to bring in some or all of the family members who are impacting on the life of the identified patient.

Boyd-Franklin (1989) mentioned that information gathering on Black families often occurs later in the treatment process. She attributed this to the process of building trust, which must be established before extensive information gathering can take place. While this may also be applicable to some immigrant families, most individuals want to get on with whatever is necessary so that they can be finished with therapy. Therefore, the therapist must determine whether the family is ready to engage in data collecting in the first session. It is important to keep in mind that with many immigrants, a therapist can establish credibility in the first few minutes of the first session merely by ascribed status.

Step 3: Determining the Stage of Acculturation

While it is important to keep in mind that not all families are really in need of therapy because of acculturation stressors, with immigrant families, difficulties in acculturation can be a major contributing factor to their family problems. Determining if there is any transitional conflict via Helms's (1985) three stages of acculturation is important in helping immigrant families. A caveat, though, is that not all families are unable to negotiate the acculturation process. Some families need therapy for the same reasons American families need therapy, for instance, the teenage rebellion typically found in any culture. In any event, once it has been determined which stage of acculturation the individual or family is in, it will be necessary to outline the goals for therapy based on the acculturation stage or any other transitional conflicts.

Step 4: Outlining the Goals

In order to further establish credibility, it is necessary, before the end of the first session, to outline concisely what the individual or family will gain; that is, the goals of therapy should be highlighted. This is to ensure that there is no discrepancy between the client's goals and the therapist's, since this can affect the therapist's credibility. As a matter of practice, at the end of every session, it is wise to reevaluate progress and see if the goals are being accomplished. Of course, even as the goals are being outlined, therapy can begin. Here again is a reminder that one advantage of this comprehensive model is that therapy can begin even while assessment is still in progress because of the cyclical nature of this treatment approach.

PHASE II: EDUCATIONAL TREATMENT PROCESS

In working with immigrant families much of therapy may be educational in nature, since many adjustment difficulties may be due to cultural differences or a lack of knowledge about the host country's educational, social, and political systems. Gopaul-McNicol, Thomas, and Irish (1991) explore basic educational and social issues of which immigrant families need to be aware and the facilities that are available to help them in the process of adjustment. Understanding the American school system, particularly the special education process (a concept foreign to many immigrant families), was examined by Thomas and Gopaul-McNicol (1991). Gopaul-McNicol (1993) suggested that if after the assessment process, it is determined that the family members lack knowledge about these basic systems, which they have to deal with every day, they may have to be educated about these systems. This stage of therapy may also involve a lot of homework, such as reading (bibliotherapy) to gain an understanding of the various systems. As can be seen, effective therapy with immigrant families requires flexibility, the use of a circular model, and even the removal of some traditional rigid boundaries. Therapists must be willing to explore the impact of the educational, social, legal, and political conditions of the families they treat. To attempt to treat these families without addressing these systems could impair the therapist's credibility.

Regarding the legal system, the next treatment stage for clients who are in this country illegally is to educate and empower them. This may involve such things as helping them find an immigration attorney or explaining their rights with respect to their children's education. This means that the therapist must know the various systems, be willing to establish contact with the different providers in these systems, and if necessary include these providers in therapy sessions.

If the assessment shows that the child is embarrassed about his/her family (a common problem many immigrant families face) because of his or her parents' accent, clothes, foods, and so forth, therapy has to focus on both the parents and the children. Parents generally feel rejected, frustrated, angry, and confused. In this stage, therapy has to focus on teaching parents the social and emotional adjustment stages that children go through. The goal of therapy is still educational at this point, since the therapist needs to assist the parents in understanding

- The causes of childhood misbehavior and the principles and concepts underlying the social learning of such behavior
- The cultural differences in values and discipline as they affect their children's adjustment
- The emotional stress and fears that emerge in a child as a result of migration and adjustment to a new family, and the difference between an emotional disturbance and cultural adjustment
- The differences in the school structure and school expectations
- The criteria used by the school system in placing children in special programs and their parental rights
- How they can build self-esteem and self-discipline in their children via a home study program, so that their children will be empowered to maintain a positive self-image in this race-conscious society
- How to communicate more effectively with their children and to be critical without affecting their child's self-esteem
- The impact of peer pressure and how it can be monitored

At this juncture, therapy will be both educational and psychological, since the children ought to be taught

- To understand the sociocultural differences between their native country and the United States (educational)
- To cope with peer taunts about their accents, mode of dressing, foods, family, and so forth (psychological)
- To communicate more effectively with their families (educational and psychological)
- To acquire the social skills and assertiveness skills needed (psychological)
- To improve study skills and to understand cultural differences in test taking, school structure, school expectations, and language factors (educational)
- To cope with the emotional stress and fears that come with migration (psychological)
- To understand the psychology of being ethnically different in American society (psychological)
- To understand the concept of self-esteem; its relation to performance and success; and the sources, institutions, and images that affect self-esteem (educational and psychological)

The assessment may reveal that the child is in Helms's stage two, the transitional phase—where the child realizes his or her lack of absolute acceptance by the White world. The individual withdraws from the dominant culture, tries to identify with his or her culture of origin, and immerses himself or herself in the values and lifestyle of that culture. This is when many adolescents begin to wear the dreadlocks, to rebel against their parents' Eurocentric view, and to talk emotionally of "Mother Africa." In other words, they do not necessarily have a true understanding and a true appreciation of their history; they identify out of rebellion, due to a loss of culture, feelings of rejection, and a need to grasp anything left of their cultural pride. This is the most difficult stage for both parents and children. They all have to acknowledge racism and discrimination. The main affect is one of frustration and anger, and behavior is generally militant. Interpersonal relations tend to become limited mainly to one's own cultural group. Therapy has to be both extensive and intensive, tapping many modalities—affective, interpersonal, educational, behavioral, cognitive, structural, and multiple systems.

If the assessment shows that the child is in the final or transcendent stage of acculturation, the client may not need psychological therapy as such (at least not for acculturation matters), because he or she has become bicultural and uses the experiences from both cultural groups to best fit his or her own circumstances. As can be seen from the above, Bowen's systems educational therapy, which views therapy as a self-change process and which portrays the therapist as a teacher (as described in the previous chapter), is quite compatible with the needs of immigrant families.

PHASE III: PSYCHOLOGICAL TREATMENT PROCESS

The greater the cultural difference between therapist and client, the greater the challenge to maintain the relationship. These cultural differences can dominate the therapeutic relationship and affect therapeutic progress. With an immigrant family the therapist's efforts to "cross over" may have to be greater than they would be with a family with similar values and customs as the therapist's. I have found that the combination of Lazarus's broad-based, multimodal approach, Minuchin's structural approach, and Bowen's family dynamics approach is the most helpful in addressing the psychological problems faced by immigrant families and in easing the "joining" or "crossing over" process. As has been demonstrated above, the initial stages of therapy with immigrant families tend to be very educational, unless there is a crisis due to some traumatic incident. However, once the individual or family is familiar with the various systems, and if the problem persists (at times therapy with immigrant families may be merely educational), then a more psychological approach to treatment is needed.

Applying Multimodal Therapy with Immigrants

Multimodal assessment with its multilayered approach focuses on behaviors that are impeding happiness and acculturation of immigrant families. The therapist will observe and ask what makes an individual sad, frightened, angry, anxious, timid, and so forth, as well as observe what type of behaviors the individual displays when feeling these emotions. Is the individual avoiding, violent, and so forth?

Generally, when maladaptive behaviors are present, behavior therapy will be implemented. Thus clients will be taught to practice prescribed exercises, be they relaxation, meditation, assertiveness training, modeling, and so forth. Behavioral contracts would be set up, whereby the client is rewarded for compliance and deprived of privileges for noncompliance. The works of Behaviorists such as Skinner (1974), Bandura (1969), Meinchenbaum (1977), and Jacobson (1938) can all be applied, depending on the nature of the problem. As mentioned above, it is highly common in multimodal therapy to begin intervening in the first interview, rather than waiting until the full assessment procedure is completed, to alleviate stress. For example, if a child says he or she is stuttering because of feeling very nervous, Jacobson's progressive relaxation can be applied in the first session. In a sense, this will seem like a "gift" to the family, because a direct relationship between therapy and alleviation of problems would have been demonstrated. The therapist's credibility would have been established as well.

There is a strong correlation among one's cognition, affect, and behaviors. How one feels (affect) to a large extent determines how one behaves or thinks. Likewise, how one thinks influences how one feels or behaves. As a result, while I agree with Brice (1982) that some culturally diverse individuals "have a covert agreement among themselves not to reveal feelings" (p. 131), I do not agree that "the therapist's efforts to amplify feelings could be threatening" (p. 131) and that therefore "questions aimed at feelings will reach a dead end" (p. 131). In my experience with immigrant families, including the men, I have seen a profound need to express feelings, once the therapist has established credibility. I recommend addressing the affective side by exploring feelings in an empathetic manner. Domokos-Cheng Ham (1989a, 1989b) discusses how the therapist can "join" with immigrant families in an empathetic manner. Essentially, the author talked about the interactive process, the diadic relationship between therapist and client, and the therapist's ability to convey emotional sensitivity. Gladstein (1983), Rogers (1975b), and Asby (1975) all emphasized the value of the therapist's listening for feelings. As researchers and academicians, we have had a tendency to look for specificity. Thus when we encounter imprecise quantities, such as feelings and empathy, we attempt to dismiss them because these abstract constructs cannot be measured. I believe that teaching a client to express affect is a process. While it is important to proceed cautiously when attempting to uncover unconscious feelings, there is no doubt that culturally different families, when faced with their children's maladaptive behaviors, express some feelings very openly. It is expressed in ways such as "I don't understand. This is not the way we behave. I feel frustrated. I am sending my child back home." What they are saying is that they cannot cope. Threatening to send the children back to their native lands (after waiting so long to be reunited with them) is the ultimate expression of pain, fear, and anger. Therapy must address these feelings, as well as teach the parents coping skills. The important factor to note here is that, while the therapist may be affectively empathetic, he or she must maintain "cognitive empathetic skills in perceiving, categorizing and making sense" of the client's feelings (Domokos-Cheng Ham, 1989a, p. 38). The idea, then, is not merely to feel what the client is feeling, but to comprehend and act on what the client is feeling. In my experience with immigrant families, affective therapy is best introduced somewhere around the middle or end of the therapeutic process. However, if the need arises earlier, the therapist should assist the client in amplifying his or her feelings.

Likewise, exploring how thoughts influence emotions and behavior, the therapist may try to examine the client's belief (cognition) systems. Examining the client's belief that his or her child "should, ought to, must" do well may help shed some light on the undue pressure that some parents sometimes place on their children, albeit unintentionally.

Albert Ellis's (1974) rational emotive therapy (RET), which is a cognitive, behavioral, and affective approach to treatment, is quite relevant to immigrant families for the following reasons:

1. It does not require the client to give up his or her values and cultural reality. Therefore, the client does not have to endorse the therapist's culture in order to get well. RET is a value-free form of therapy because it helps the client to achieve his or her goals within his or her own sociocultural context. Problems usually arise when the client's new belief system is in conflict with his or her cultural belief system. Thus a client who no longer shares the views of his or her traditional culture may experience cognitive dissonance, which has to be worked through. In such a case, the client can be taught that it is not so "awful" if his or her goals or values have to be changed in order to function in this society. Similarly, the client can be taught that maintaining his or her traditional values is also acceptable.

2. It is proactive, short-term, and goal-directed.

3. It provides the client with a link among his or her thoughts, affect, and behavior.

4. Rational beliefs are logical. Therefore, when a client believes, for instance, that coming to the United States has destroyed his manhood, he is made to recognize through RET that manhood is not so fragile a concept that any event can destroy it. The important thing to keep in mind is that through this cognitive approach to therapy, many of a client's irrational thoughts can be examined. Therefore, parents who simply expect their children to like the cultural change merely because they did, or to do well because the opportunity is here, or to acculturate with minimal difficulty can benefit from Ellis's rational emotive therapy.

Interpersonal relations is the area in which immigrant children experience the most difficulty in school. McNicol (1991) outlined, from a child's perspective, several areas of adjustment that children go through when they are reunited with their families. Many children fall at each end of the continuum—unassertiveness leading to withdrawal or aggression leading to violence or disruptive behavior. Teaching alternative ways of coping with problem situations via role play, assertiveness training, and social-skills training should aid in addressing this problem. In addition, teaching children to cope with peer taunts and helping them to understand the sociocultural differences between their native countries and the United States are some ways in improving their interpersonal relationships.

In order to improve poor self-esteem (a problem commonly seen in immigrant children), it can be helpful to explore how they perceive themselves and their body, with questions such as "What do you dislike or like about yourself?" then observing how these self-images influence their moods, sensations, and behaviors. The child may persistently complain about unpleasant sensations, such as aches and pains. Often this is the child's way of communicating stress in dealing with the cultural transition. Cognitive/behavior therapy will address the child's anxieties, but parents also have to be taught how not to reinforce or cultivate the anxiety by allowing the child to skip school. Whenever immigrant parents come into conflict with the school system, an option they tend to consider is keeping the child out of school for a few days, hoping the problem will simply disappear when they return. Many of them are unaware of terms and realities such as educational neglect, and such concepts must be taught to them. What can be seen in examining the multimodal approach to therapy is that when dealing with behavior, affect, sensation, imagery, cognition, and interpersonal factors, the emphasis is essentially educational. The therapist offers guidance, displays caring, modifies faulty styles, corrects misconceptions, provides information, and delivers the support necessary for the client to attain his or her goals.

In selecting which problems and which modality to address first, Lazarus (1976) recommends starting with the most obvious problem and using the most logical procedure. This will overcome the penchant for making straightforward problems needlessly complicated.

Systems (Educational) Approach

Bowen's (1978) systems approach emphasizes the importance of communicating strategically within the family context. His concept of the "coach" is very applicable in working with immigrant families. Rather than meeting with the family, Bowen has the person who came to therapy coach other family members into emotionally mature relationships with one another. I have found this "coaching" approach very helpful, because it is so difficult to get an entire family to come into therapy. Since the men are so resistant and tend to deny the therapist adequate entry, using a coach may be the next most effective approach. In addition, the term "family therapy" can be quite threatening to some immigrant families, who may surmise that the entire family is being seen as dysfunctional. Bowen's "coaching," which makes it unnecessary for the entire family to be present simultaneously, is also useful because parents often have difficulty engaging in discussions in the presence of their children, which is the typical mode of family therapy. If this technique is used, members who may not have otherwise become involved in therapy may be treated. I have found that the best coach is the eldest male child. While the mother is traditionally the intermediary between the father and the children, in the final analysis, she is expected to side with the father, especially in the presence of the children. The eldest son, by virtue of being a male and an elder offspring, is the one who can gain the respect of the younger siblings (because he himself is still in cultural transition), as well as get the attention of his parents, especially his father, because of his seniority in the hierarchical family structure. Bowen's interview technique of instructing family members to attend to one another and distinguish between thoughts and feelings is helpful in fostering more constructive contact between father and son or mother and daughter. His emphasis on the person-to-person relationship (the relationship each family member has with one another), has been helpful in counteracting the vulnerability that individual members feel when the entire family is against one family member. Moreover, Bowen's technique of tracing multigenerational emotional patterns helps to differentiate the individual, since he or she can confront the family's arbitrary rules with a defined sense of self.

In addition, I have found Bowen's emphasis on personal responsibility and respect for individual boundaries very appealing to adolescents. Many adolescents who are attempting to distance themselves from their families through individuation and differentiation welcome this shifting of the family process to their own individuality. However, the therapist ought to be mindful of the deeply rooted importance of the family for many culturally diverse people. Therefore, using the approach of creating distance from family may make the individual at a later point feel shallow in spite of his or her attempts at independence. It is best to encourage members to negotiate their individuation within the family. I have found that individuals much more readily embrace a feeling of reconnection to their families that allows some level of independence. Therefore distancing, as discussed by Bowen, should not take the form of complete differentiation from the family, but should emphasize maintaining family contacts, while advocating emotional expressiveness with the families. The therapist has to teach the client to be prepared at each stage of differentiation to deal with his or her family's reaction, which may be feelings of rejection and betrayal. Moreover, the Bowenian systems model does fit immigrant families in that it emphasizes self-determination, a concept very much endorsed in most societies around the world.

Structural Approach

Minuchin's (1974) structural family therapy approach, which emphasizes hierarchies within the family, is very relevant to many cultural groups. Parents and grandparents are usually in favor of Minuchin's emphasis on generational boundaries, instead of approaches that emphasize equal rights for all family members. By actively restructuring the family interactions, rather than relying on expressions of feelings to create change, Minuchin helps to realign the family's boundaries. This approach is particularly helpful in aiding in the process of acculturation, since Minuchin emphasizes that the individual's symptoms are due to the family's failure to accommodate its structure to the changing environmental requirements. Like many first-generation immigrants, many people from varying cultural backgrounds have difficulty "letting go" and endorsing the concept of biculturalism.

Minuchin's approach helps the parents recognize that the children need to become involved in American society in order to assimilate with minimal difficulty. Therefore, when therapy challenges the family structure, the family is moved to examine the enmeshment syndrome that may be impeding cultural adjustment. In addition, Minuchin's use of the extended family as an integral component of therapy is very effective with immigrants, since the extended family plays a pivotal role in family life.

PHASE IV: EMPOWERMENT TREATMENT PROCESS

The empowering of the family via a multisystems approach is the final stage of treatment. Boyd-Franklin (1989) examines the importance of intervening at various levels—individual, family, extended family, church, community, and social services. There is little doubt that this approach can be quite effective, because it provides a flexible set of guidelines for intervention with immigrant families. Encouraging the individual to embrace the support of his or her extended family and nonblood kin in areas such as child care and education may help in preventing personal difficulties. The use of the church in therapy with immigrants is also very relevant, because of the importance religion plays in the life of most immigrant families. The church can serve as a valuable social service in times of crisis, particularly for single parents. The therapist should suggest the church as a support system and even seek permission from the family to talk to the priest or minister in attempting to ascertain what role the church can play in the therapeutic process. Of course, it is also important for the therapist to recognize the significant influence of the folk beliefs in many religious societies. Leininger (1973) recommended using both indigenous practitioner skills and professional practices. I do not believe it is necessary for the therapists to conduct spiritual counseling or even to have a referral list for practitioners of witchcraft, since one has to be knowledgeable to venture into this form of treatment and comfortable with this procedure to make such a referral. However, it is necessary for therapists to understand that their opposition to the family's seeking the help of such practitioners may impede the psychotherapeutic process. I have always provided emotional support to my clients who felt they were victims of bewitchment and asked them to keep me abreast of what happened after their visits to the spiritists.

Also critical is that the therapist must help the family find out what after-school programs exist in their communities, since allegations of neglect are sometimes brought against working parents whose young children are at home alone after school. The families need to be taught that this is frowned upon in American society and that child-care programs can be used. Boyd-Franklin (1989) recommended that therapists should keep a file on these different services so they can mobilize them when necessary. This kind of tapping of available resources is sometimes the single most important interaction in facilitating the possibility of treatment.

In addition, the therapist needs to be knowledgeable about the legal system as it applies to immigration policies and to be familiar with at least one immigration attorney, because of the illegal immigration status of many immigrant families. The

American Immigration Lawyers' Association can provide a list of names to help in obtaining the name of an attorney from the individual's cultural background. Knowing about the immigration laws is important both in order to be sensitive to the family's fears surrounding their immigrant status and also to be able to help them with specific information—for example, that children cannot be denied a public education because of their immigrant status, a fact of which most culturally different families are unaware.

The MULTI-CMS approach also recognizes that within communities, the idea that "it takes a whole community to raise a child" is fully endorsed by many people around the world. Immigrant families are generally not aware of the various systems (educational, legal, community), and empowering them to use all of the support systems available to them is crucial to the acculturation process. The use of these systems can be implemented at any stage in therapy, but the families must be aware of all potential systems before therapy is terminated so that they can readily tap into them if the need arises.

In general, in using the MULTI-CMS approach to treating immigrant families, a therapist can explore a broad spectrum of techniques to address the needs of this population. The following cases show how this comprehensive approach can be practically implemented.

10
Case Samples
with the MULTI-CMS Approach

A HAITIAN FAMILY

Marie, a thirty-three-year-old Haitian woman, was referred for psychotherapy because she was given a dual diagnosis of clinical depression and paranoid schizophrenia by a psychiatrist. According to the referring information, her two children (ages eleven and seven) were taken away from her because she was said to be a "neglectful parent" who left her children at home unsupervised. The psychiatrist noted that Marie repeatedly complained of chest pains, had difficulty sleeping at night, and constantly made reference to a spirit that talked to her every night to warn her that "someone is doing me evil through voodoo because they are jealous of me." The psychiatrist felt that her hearing of voices and seeing of spirits were symptoms of paranoid schizophrenia. The psychiatrist in his report also noted that a French psychologist had diagnosed Marie as retarded, because upon arrival in the United States as a "boat person," she was given an IQ test in French and fell within the retarded range.

Of note in the referring information are the school reports which reflected both academic and behavioral difficulties of her seven-year-old son. Moreover, the school psychologist noted belt marks on the child's right arm. This was reported to Child Protective Services, where the referral was originated.

Before treatment had begun, it was recommended that Marie see a medical doctor to rule out any physical problems. The results revealed no medical problems that warranted any special medical care. The report attributed her chest pains to emotional stress.

Initial Session

The initial session met with resistance since Marie felt that she did not need treatment, because like many Haitians, she felt that "if I have a problem, I don't need a shrink. I can resolve the problem on my own." The interview with the therapist revealed that there were many misconceptions about treatment and they were cleared up in the first session (explaining the process of treatment—Phase I, Step 1-A of the MULTI-CMS approach). The concept of psychotherapy, the role of a psychologist, and the potential gains that can be made from treatment were all clearly explained and discussed. After about thirty minutes, Marie was not as resistant when she realized therapy was not for "crazy people" only.

In the first session, after greeting the family, the therapist asked Marie to outline the problem as she understood it. Much anger was noted as Marie said that she was described as "a luni" by the psychiatrist because she simply said that a spirit spoke to her. Because the therapist understood her cultural belief and knew that this explanation was not surprising since the Haitian culture usually attributes physical illnesses to evil doings, Marie felt understood and safe to express her feelings about her cultural belief. Within minutes of the first session Marie had received a "gift" from the therapist because "you understand me and respect my culture." Thus the therapist's credibility (Phase I, Step 1-B of the MULTI-CMS) was established in the very first session.

Likewise, Step 2 of Phase I of the MULTI-CMS approach had begun from the moment Marie felt she could trust the therapist, since she was more relaxed in divulging information about her family background and so on. It must be emphasized that the therapist was not of Haitian background.

To address the issue of her spiritual explanation for her physical illness, she was encouraged to go to a spiritual healer if she felt that a spirit was put on her. This suggestion was made as a form of respect for her cultural belief. Although she said she would not go at that time, the suggestion by the therapist resulted in her being more trusting of the therapeutic relationship. At this point she became more accepting of the explanation for her depression, which is that she was overwhelmed with responsibility since she was used to spousal support which was no longer available since her arrival in the United States.

Another possible explanation of her emotional stress was her experiences in Haiti. For newly arrived immigrants, it is important to recognize that due to the ongoing political turmoil in Haiti, many Haitians enter the United States in a state of traumatic stress. Where possible, they should be referred to support services in their neighboring communities. Her depression was stemming from the aftermath of the trauma in her native country. In essence, she was experiencing some signs of posttraumatic stress disorder. Stress management with emphasis on the cognitive/behavioral component of multimodal therapy was taught to Marie (Phase III, psychological treatment process). This was done in the very first session, in which Marie was taught relaxation therapy and given relaxation exercises to practice at home. A relaxation tape was also given to her so she could practice these exercises before bedtime since she had difficulty sleeping at night. Before the end of the first session, the goals for treatment were outlined as follows:

1. Refer her five-year-old son to an after-school program, so that he can receive the academic remediation he needs.

2. Teach Marie alternative ways of disciplining her children, so that she will not engage in corporal punishment.

3. Teach Marie about the dos and don'ts of the American social system, so that she will understand the concept of neglect when a child under age fourteen is left home alone.

4. Refer Marie to various community programs, such as the church and the employment agencies, where she can receive assistance in child care and in securing employment.

5. Have Marie be assessed by a Haitian psychologist who speaks Haitian Creole, since French is distinctly different from Haitian Creole, the dialect Marie speaks and spoke upon entry into the United States, when she was diagnosed as mentally retarded.

After the goals were outlined, Marie was referred to an after-school program near her home. Her son was offered free tutorial services. She was so excited that she had received a "gift" (Phase I, Step 1-B of the MULTI-CMS approach) from the therapist that she immediately committed to treatment for eight more weeks.

Subsequent Sessions

The second and third sessions involved teaching Marie alternative ways of disciplining her children and the dos and don'ts of the American social systems (Phase II, educational treatment process). In these two sessions, the therapist educated the family as to the social, legal, and cultural differences with respect to disciplinary methods between the United States and their native country, Haiti. The family was given some literature as to what constitutes child abuse and was asked to read it at home and discuss it in the next session. Subsequent sessions focused on educating the family about the principles of behaviorism, so alternatives to child abuse could be developed at home.

In session four, Marie was reassessed by a Haitian psychologist. A review of the culturally sensitive, nonbiased, bio-ecological approach to assessment revealed that Marie was not retarded, but rather had little formal education prior to coming to the United States. In other words she was educationally deprived. Potential intellectual functioning revealed borderline to low average potential in intelligence. A vocational assessment was conducted by the therapist, which revealed that Marie was interested in being a nurse.

In the fifth session, Marie was referred to the health education department, where she enrolled in a nurse's aide course, so she can be more self-supportive.

Phase III, the psychological treatment process, had begun from the moment treatment began, since Marie was encouraged during every session to address her feelings of loneliness, fear of never seeing her spouse, whom she left behind in Haiti, and fear of being a single parent. Sessions six to ten, however, focused exclusively on emotional and psychological issues. Thus the emotional stress and fears both children and adults experience as a result of migration and ways in which parents can build self-esteem, assertiveness skills, and study skills in their children were some of the psychological and emotional issues addressed. Multimodal therapy (Phase III) was the psychological treatment of choice. Marie was taught communications skills, behavioral contracting, and expressing affect (all part of the multimodal therapy). Recognizing how she was psychosomatizing her emotional problems as evidenced by her physical ailments further highlighted the sensation component of multimodal therapy.

The eleventh and twelfth sessions focused on further empowering Marie through community support both for herself and her children. The Haitian Community Center in a neighboring community was contacted and they served as a sort of extended family support where Marie was able to socialize on a weekend. Marie was also referred to an attorney who addressed the issue of legalizing her status to ensure that her spouse can join her in the near future.

Therapy ended after twelve sessions and all goals were met. A follow-up six months later revealed that Marie is now a nurse's aide, that her children are doing fine, and that no reports from Child Protective Services have been filed since. The Child Protective Services worker was planning on closing the case in a few weeks.

A WEST INDIAN FAMILY

The following case example is a practical illustration of the MULTI-CMS approach to therapy with a family from the English-speaking Caribbean.

The Matthews family was referred for therapy by the school psychologist due to the academic and behavioral problems of their two sons, Michael and Kendall, ages seven and nine respectively. The eldest child, Taiesha, age thirteen, was also having academic difficulties, since she was failing all courses except gymnastics. Mr. Matthews is originally from Jamaica and Mrs. Matthews is from Trinidad and Tobago. They had met in Jamaica, where Mrs. Matthews spent two years after completing high school in Trinidad. They have been married for fourteen years, although eight years after they married, Mrs. Matthews migrated to the United States "for a better life and to give my children the chance to get a good education." The children lived in Jamaica with their father and paternal grandparents. Michael was one year old when his mother left home, Kendall was three, and Taiesha was seven. Since Mrs. Matthews had come to the United States on a holiday visa, but had decided to stay on doing domestic work, she had lived for three years illegally in this country. In that time, she was unable to visit her children in Jamaica because she would not have been allowed reentry into the United States. She was later sponsored by her employer and obtained permanent residency (approximately five years after leaving home). She immediately sponsored her family, who are now here. Although they are not legal permanent residents yet, she expects them to become so within the next few months. When the family joined Mrs. Matthews the children were then six, eight, and twelve. Currently the household is comprised of the nuclear family, a maternal aunt and uncle, and the maternal grandmother. The children have not seen the paternal grandparents, with whom they lived since they left Jamaica.

These background data were sent by the school psychologist along with the referring information. In addition, there are allegations of possible child abuse and educational neglect due to the children's excessive absences from school. School officials are strongly considering placing both boys in special education due to emotional disturbances and Taiesha in special education due to a learning disability. However, they agreed to withhold special education placement until psychotherapeutic intervention occurred.

Initial Session

As had been agreed on the telephone, all members of the nuclear family came in for the first session. The therapist, having greeted the family, began the treatment process by asking the parents to discuss the problem as they understood it. Mrs. Matthews looked frustrated because Mr. Matthews was very angry that the family "had to be seen as crazy and abusive." He sat away from the rest of the family and did not say anything for the first fifteen minutes. Mrs. Matthews explained much of what was mentioned in the referral, and the children were generally quiet. The therapist (who was a young, female clinical psychologist) initially found it necessary to address some of the family's misconceptions about the range of clients who seek counseling. The therapist also agreed with Mr. Matthews that many families are labeled abusive when in fact they are using culturally sanctioned ways of disciplining their children. At this juncture, Mr. Matthews "joined" with the therapist by sharing his frustration with this system. By conceptualizing the problem in a manner consistent with the family's cultural experiences and beliefs, the therapist gained credibility with Mr. Matthews. The therapist also used this session to enlighten the family about some basic social and cultural differences, such as sleeping arrangements, educational neglect, and the meaning of child abuse in American society. Sensitivity to the children's presence was taken into consideration, since the therapist wanted to respect the hierarchical order of family life structure and not reveal too much in the presence of the children. Both Mr. and Mrs. Matthews said at the end of the session how much they had learned about educational, social, and cultural differences. The therapist had given to the family a "gift," and the family had already seen the therapist as "credible" after the first session. The therapeutic process was explained, and the family agreed to give therapy a chance for at least one month.

Gathering Information and Outlining Goals

Both the first and the second sessions were spent gathering information, as well as engaging in the treatment process. The Comprehensive Assessment Battery (Gopaul-McNicol, 1993) was used as a guide. The second session was quite enlightening, since several issues were revealed as problems within the family:

- Mr. Matthews's unemployment
- The children's feeling that they did not belong in the school and that their parents did not understand them

- Taiesha's embarrassment about her parents' accent and cultural values
- The maternal grandmother's attitude toward her son-in-law because her daughter was now the breadwinner (working two jobs)
- The spanking of all the children by extended family members
- The parents' belief that Taiesha "had gotten rude"
- The endorsement of the folk belief that "it is possible someone in Jamaica envied us because they heard we were doing well and put something on the children"
- The fear that the children "will be deported home if they continue to give trouble in school"

The therapist continued to engage in the treatment process by explaining the educational and legal rights of the family. At the end of the session, the family was also given homework—reading two handbooks for immigrants on the educational and social systems and on special education. At the end of this session, some goals were outlined, which included empowering the family to use the educational support systems in their communities in order to help the children in math and reading. The therapist also supported the family's decision to visit a spiritist by asking to be kept abreast of the results of their meetings with the obeah practitioner. In the meantime (during session interim), the therapist sent a letter to the school explaining to the principal that supplemental instruction in the English language might prove to be beneficial for all of the children. Goals also involved teaching all adults in the household alternative ways of disciplining children, as well as examining the effect of family role change on the family's stability.

Empowerment through the Extended Family and the Educational and Psychological Treatment Processes

There was much resistance on the part of the extended family toward coming in for treatment because they did not think that the problems with the children were caused by them. Therefore, the therapist suggested making a home visit. Thus the third session of family therapy was conducted at home. As agreed, the entire family was at home upon the therapist's arrival. The family was more responsive to therapy being conducted in the home. In addressing the resistance, the therapist did not agree or disagree with the extended family's attitude that they did not need therapy but rather spoke of contributions family members could make in helping to solve the problem. Resistance was diminished considerably, in that each family member explored ways in which he or she could be of more assistance. The aunt and uncle agreed to help in the areas of remediation and in spending more time with the children. This session also focused briefly on what constitutes child abuse. Extended family members recognized that they had been unaware of the legal ramifications of engaging in corporal punishment. Subsequent sessions with the adults were also educational in nature, in that the focus was on the emotional stress that children experience as a result of migration and their concomitant shift in value orientation.

The differences in the school structure and expectations, test-taking styles, and so forth were all examined.

By this time, the family had agreed to continue with therapy for another month, and the extended family members had agreed to come into the clinic. At this juncture both family therapy and group therapy were being provided on a weekly basis. From the fourth session up to the end of therapy, Michael and Kendall joined a group for young boys, while Taiesha joined a group for teenage girls. In both groups, issues such as coping with peer pressure, social skills and assertiveness training (to assist with interpersonal relations), building self-esteem, understanding the educational differences in test-taking styles, and coping with their fears about acculturation were addressed. In addition, Michael and Kendall were taught self-control separate from the group, while Taiesha's embarrassment around her parents' accent and her father's refusal to treat her as a teenager were discussed in a family session.

Family therapy was held with the adults only to address the conflict as a result of family role changes. The children were asked to sit outside when marital issues were being discussed. Mr. and Mrs. Matthews both felt that having the children sit in on the therapy session would result in their knowing about marital conflicts. This wish was respected, but Mrs. Matthews's mother, who was also a catalyst in creating stress on Mr. Matthews, was expected to be in attendance. Rational emotive therapy explored their cultural beliefs about men being the sole breadwinners. In addition, the role conflict for children and parents was addressed in family therapy by helping family members to establish some individuation, but at the same time maintaining family cohesiveness. Group therapy for Taiesha also addressed how adolescents can prepare their families at each stage of the differentiation process. Furthermore, group therapy focused on helping Taiesha to understand her parents' perception of the hierarchies within the family and what it means in relation to respect.

In addition, the family was taught the principles of behaviorism and how they may have directly or indirectly reinforced negative behaviors in one another. A behavior modification program was set up at home, whereby the children were reinforced for good behavior and effort in school. After obtaining the parents' informed consent, the therapist sent the teachers letters explaining what was being done and how it would be helpful for them to send home the daily behavior checklist so that the family could appropriately reward the children. The children were then further rewarded by the therapist during group therapy time.

It was not until around the sixth family session that the children's feelings of not being loved by their family were addressed. The children's feelings about their father's "abuses" and their mother's extended hours at work were also discussed. Kendall was particularly emotional as he talked about not feeling loved because his father never hugged him. This session focused on touching as a form of communicating, and everyone was asked to hug the nearest person. Then everyone was told to hug whichever family members he or she so desired. Interestingly, no one reached to hug Mr. Matthews until it was pointed out by the therapist. At that point, he said he would like to hug everyone and proceeded to do so. From that session onward, homework involved daily tactile forms of communication. In the meantime, the reality of Mrs. Matthews needing to work in order to pay the bills was explored, but all family members decided they would assist in domestic matters so that she would be free to engage in family activities once she got home. Mr. Matthews, who had refused to cook before, agreed to do so, so that Mrs. Matthews would not have to get up early to cook before leaving for work. In addition, Mr. Matthews agreed to enroll in an educational program to obtain his high school diploma while still seeking employment.

The ninth session in treatment was educational again, since family members were encouraged to establish contact with more social support systems. Taiesha joined a youth group that was monitored by West Indian adults in the community. She built a wonderful network of friends who had themselves gone through cultural conflicts while in transition. Mr. Matthews eventually agreed to join a Black male self-esteem group, which focused on such issues as "the invisibility syndrome" as it pertains to Black males and the psychology of being a Black male in this society. All family members agreed to become members of their local church. The therapist established contact with the pastor, who introduced the family to the congregation at Mass.

In the meantime, the children continued to show academic delays, but behavior problems had decreased considerably. The therapist visited the school with the parents and suggested at a school-based support team meeting what each discipline (psychologist, nurse, social worker, teacher) could be responsible for in assisting these children. While this was a difficult task, given the bureaucracy in the education system, the team members did agree to refrain from placing the children in special education for at least two years.

The success of this case may be a result of the holistic approach to therapy. The MULTI-CMS approach, while demanding, covered all areas that caused distress within the family unit. In addition, the concept "it takes a whole community to raise a child" certainly aided this family in arming and empowering themselves as they attempted to acculturate to American society.

PART IV

TRAINING IMPLICATIONS

11
A Theoretical Framework for Training Therapists to Use the MULTI-CMS Model: An Exploration of the Major Competencies

THE CHALLENGE FACING PSYCHOLOGY

One of the major challenges facing the field of psychology today is the training of therapists to address the psychological needs of the increasing number of linguistically and culturally diverse families here in the United States (Barona et al., 1990; "High Achieving," 1985; Reid, 1986; U.S. Department of Commerce, 1989). The fact that there continues to be a high drop-out rate and a low academic achievement rate for minority children makes this situation even more acute. Since it is virtually impossible to have an equal number of trained specialists who are themselves from the variety of culturally diverse backgrounds as the client population is, it is critically important to have the graduates of psychology training programs be knowledgeable about, and be prepared to address, the concerns of this new clientele. Unless this is addressed, psychology will continue to result in outcomes antithetical to the spirit of the mission of the profession. Of course, multicultural training of all psychologists ought not to mitigate the efforts of psychology programs to simultaneously recruit ethnic and culturally different minority students. The goal should really be to train all psychologists to be competent, sensitive, and knowledgeable of the critical factors related to issues of cultural diversity in order to best serve the culturally different. This knowledge, sensitivity, and awareness ought to be built into the existing psychology training programs.

Throughout this book many assessment and counseling skills are suggested in working with immigrant families. While those are all strongly recommended, other competencies are needed as prerequisites to best utilize the MULTI-CMS model. The primary purpose of this chapter is to propose major competency skills that are needed by all therapists to function as effective helpers.

MAJOR COMPETENCIES NEEDED FOR
MULTICULTURAL/MULTIMODAL/MULTISYSTEMS TRAINING

A number of researchers (Barona et al., 1990; Carney & Kahn, 1984; Casas et al., 1986; Cummins, 1989; Figueroa et al., 1984; Hills & Strozier, 1992; Kiselica, 1991; McRae & Johnson, 1991; Palmer et al., 1991; Ponterotto & Casas, 1987; Ridley, 1985; Rogers et al., 1992; Sabnani et al., 1991; Sue et al., 1992) have highlighted some of the necessary competencies for psychologists to acquire in working with culturally diverse clients. Table 11.1 summarizes the major multicultural competencies most needed to effectively service clients from diverse cultural backgrounds.

Cross-Cultural Ethical Competence

The basis for a specialization in multicultural training for all psychologists grew out of the needs of minorities throughout various systems. The fundamental premise underlying this position is that the treatment of culturally diverse clients by professionals who lack the specialized training and expertise is unethical, since this is considered delivery of mental health services outside one's area of competence (American Psychological Association, 1981; Fields, 1979; Korman, 1974; Ridley, 1985). Thus cross-cultural skill ought to be on a level of parity with other specialized assessment and therapeutic skills. Acceptance of this perspective suggests that a higher and more profound level of training is needed if cross-cultural competence is to be acquired. The key issue to note is that minority students should not be the sole beneficiaries of cross-cultural training. Oftentimes, White professionals even more than minority professionals are involved in making critical decisions on the lives of minority clientele. Thus it is necessary to keep in mind that at the heart of this ethical imperative is the welfare of the client.

Therapist's Awareness of Own Cultural Biases and Values

Arredondo et al. (1996) suggested that all psychologists in training should explore their fundamental significant beliefs and attitudes and the impact of those beliefs on the psychological processes and on their ability to respect others different from themselves. They should be allowed to examine their values that impede respect of others' values and beliefs. The adage "counselor know thyself" is critical in preventing ethnocentrism in cross-cultural counseling. Culturally competent psychologists ought to be trained to recognize, in a teaching or counseling relationship, how and when their beliefs, attitudes, and values interfere with providing the best service to their clients. Likewise, training should allow them to recognize the limits of their skills and to know when to refer the client to receive more appropriate resources. Training should have at its heart the ability to recognize the sources of discomfort or comfort with respect to differences in culture, ethnicity, and so on, and how these differences are played out in therapy. A culturally competent psychologist is one who tries to avoid making negative judgments on his or her clients even if their worldview differs from that of the counselor. In other words, culturally competent psychologists respect and appreciate their clients' differences.

Competence in Understanding Interracial Issues

Race is a rather perplexing and elusive aspect of life in the United States (Carter, 1995). When a Black person introduces race into psychotherapy, it is often perceived as a form of defense or as an avoidance of a more profound issue. Given the U.S. preoccupation with race in the sociopolitical world, it is imperative that students in training are exposed to a psychotherapeutic model that includes race (Carter, 1995). Issues discussed should include the following: whether the therapist should wait for the client to introduce questions of race, how race should be discussed once the issue has arisen, what ways there are in which racial factors may influence the course of treatment, and how one can distinguish between a racial defense and poor psychological functioning. Moreover, knowledge of racial oppression and racial discrimination should be examined in training, so that White therapists can recognize how they benefit from institutionalized and cultural racism.

Cross-Cultural Awareness

Figueroa et al. (1984) emphasized the importance of acquiring awareness of the variations of different cultural groups with respect to motivational and learning styles, expectations related to achievement, exceptionality, and family roles. Medway (1995) emphasized the importance of psychologists being aware of the impact of migration and relocation. Oftentimes there are many stresses associated with environmental change, such as financial pressures and unemployment. It may well be necessary for the psychologist to spend some time in the child's ecology to fully appreciate the experiential aspect to this, so that this cross-cultural knowledge can be applied in psychological assessment, treatment plans, decisions on retention and placement, and so on. Sue and Sue (1990) states that a culturally competent psychologist is one who is actively in the process of becoming aware of his or her own assumptions about human behavior.

Language Competencies

While it is necessary for a psychologist to be proficient in the language of a client who only speaks his/her native language, for clients who are more proficient in English, bilingual proficiency on the part of the therapist is not a necessity. Certainly the therapist's competency in the oral and written skills of the client makes it easier for the therapist to establish rapport with the client, and enables the client to express his/her feelings more fluidly. Being bilingually proficient also allows the examiner to alternate language as needed and even to be sensitive to dialectical differences. Moreover, being a native speaker of a particular language and being familiar with a client's culture also afford the examiner an awareness of subtleties in nonverbal communicative cues. There is no question that being bilingual is preferred, but since

Table 11.1

Major Multicultural Competencies for Working with Culturally Diverse Children

1. Cross-Cultural Ethical Competence
   - the treatment of culturally diverse clients by professionals who lack the specialized training and expertise is unethical
2. Awareness of the Therapist's own Values and Biases
   - knowledge regarding the therapist's own racial heritage and how it professionally affects the therapeutic process
   - knowledge of how oppression and discrimination personally affect the therapist and his/her work
3. Cross-Cultural Awareness
   - acquiring awareness of the variations of different cultural groups with respect to motivational and learning styles, family roles, and the impact of migration and relocation
4. Competence in Understanding Interracial Issues
   - issues such as whether the therapist should wait for the client to introduce questions of race
   - what are some ways that racial factors may influence the course of treatment
5. Language Competencies
   - learn to work with bilingual clients either through the use of interpreters or by learning a second language
6. Acquiring Competency in the Ability to Work with Interpreters
   - knowledge of interpretation procedures—establishing rapport with the interpreters
   - respecting the authority of the interpreter
   - knowing the kinds of information that tend to get lost during the interpretation procedure
   - recognizing the importance of securing accurate translation
7. Cross-Cultural Assessment Competencies
   - can use assessment instruments appropriately with groups for whom the tests were not standardized
   - can articulate the limitations of the instrument with various groups
8. Cross-Cultural Counseling Competencies
   - respect the indigenous helping beliefs and practices
   - aware of the institutional impediments that hinder the use of counseling services
9. Cross-Cultural Issues in Conflict Resolution
   - it is necessary for the counselor to help the client to identify the ways in which conflicts affect therapy
10. Competence in Special Education Prevention
11. Competencies in Knowing the Bilingual Education Curriculum
    - knowing what constitutes a bilingual instructional program

Table 11.1 (continued)

12. Cross-Cultural Consultation Competencies
- they are not adverse to seeking consultation with religious healers
- consult with heads of organizations that focus on providing services to individuals of different cultural groups

13. Cross-Cultural Research Competencies
- familiarize themselves with relevant research regarding the mental health of various ethnic and racial groups
- identify research that is conducted by respected professionals and viewed as credible by community members

14. Competence in Empowering Families through Community-Based Organizations
15. Competence in Pediatric/Health Psychology
16. Competence in Parent Training

---

it is impossible for a psychologist to learn all of the 120 languages that are commonly found in some of the metropolitan areas, it is best for all psychologists to be trained in a number of competencies. A psychologist who has been trained in understanding cultural diversity, in working with interpreters, in ecological assessment, and in integrating language proficiency data in report writing can be quite capable of assessing an individual who is from a bilingual home, but is more proficient and dominant in English. Therefore, using a therapist with limited bilingual ability should not be ruled out.

In addition, culturally skilled psychologists should possess knowledge about the differences in communication styles and how these different styles of communication may clash with those of their clients.

An even greater obstacle in working with linguistically different clients is the impact of dialectical differences on the examinee's performance. "Dialects can pose serious difficulties for the psychologist in understanding the full meaning of clients' responses" (Figueroa et al., 1984, p. 136). Children from some English-speaking-countries such as Jamaica speak with an English Creole—an amalgamation of English, French, Spanish, and African languages. Therefore, while these children read and write in English, they speak in a Creole dialect. They may say "him say," but will write "he says." In a testing situation, if examiners are not knowledgeable of the dialectical variants, they may assume a speech impediment and may misdiagnose the child as speech impaired—a rather common diagnosis given to children who are English-speaking immigrants. A competent psychologist should at least be in the position to ask the question as to whether dialectical factors may be affecting the child's performance. Such children tend to need, not English as a second language (ESL) services, but English as a second dialect (ESD) (Coelho, 1991; Gopaul-McNicol, 1993). Thus the focus should be on more opportunities for conversation than on basic interpersonal communication skills involving intensive instruction in vocabulary and grammar, so characteristic of ESL programs. Children who require ESD services need more opportunity for oral stimulation in the mainstream dialect where the emphasis is on social appropriateness. In other words these children simply have to be taught to "discriminate in which situations each dialect will serve them most effectively" (Coelho, 1976, p. 37).

A competent psychologist should be able to apply the information gathered from the clinical interview, family interview, assessment, behavioral observations, and so on, in determining a child's proficiency in a language. If the psychologist only taps the school domain and ignores the home and the community, then a child who has had little or no exposure to school vocabulary in his/her native or second language may appear alingual, that is, possessing little proficiency in either language. In developing an adequate program for language remediation, the psychologist must be knowledge-able of the kinds of conditions that impede or facilitate learning a second language and should aid in creating such an environment for the child. Thus knowledge of the normal course of language acquisition for monolingual children, bilingual children, issues of motivation, and so on, ought to be discussed with the teacher and parent. A well-documented understanding of these issues can be found in Homel et al., (1987).

Acquiring Competency in the Ability to Work with Interpreters

In spite of every effort to secure a bilingual psychologist, at times it is impossible to do so, given the paucity of bilingual psychologists who speak "exotic" languages that are not so commonly encountered. As such, it is neces-sary for psychologists to develop competencies in the interpretation procedures. Some of these skills can range from establishing rapport with the interpreters, respecting the authority of the interpreter, even if the interpreter is a teacher's aide/paraprofessional or a member of the Parent-Teacher Association (PTA), knowing the kinds of information that tend to get lost during the interpretation procedure, understanding nonverbal communication clues, and recognizing the importance of securing accurate translation. Also evident should be knowl-edge of translations that are not a result of personal evaluation by the inter-preter. Moreover, "the psychologist should demonstrate the ability to plan and execute preservice and in-service programs to prepare interpreters for psycho-logical work with children and to help interpreters follow ethical practices of keeping information confidential" (Figueroa et al., 1984, p. 138). It must be emphasized that unlike in a legal context, testing an individual is a more complex role for the interpreter. In the world of psychology nonverbal cues can be misinterpreted if the interpreter is not familiar with the client's culture. The psychologist must ensure that kinesthetic cues are not misinterpreted by the interpreter. Figueroa et al., (1984) recommended the use of audio tapes or videotapes to address this situation, since a precise recording of the testing can be reviewed by the psychologist after completion of the testing.

Cross-Cultural Assessment Competencies

Critical to the assessment of culturally different clients, as was discussed in Part I of this text, is "the ability to judge the appropriateness of the instrument selected on the basis of psychometric and linguistic criteria" (Figueroa et al., 1984, p. 135). Thus there must be consideration given to reliability, validity, standards for administration, test interpretation, and test limitations—both cognitive as well as socioemotional factors in the assessment procedures. The important issue to note is when sociocultural factors may be impeding the assessment process. To control for this it is advised to not limit oneself to formal assessment only. Using only traditional, formal assessment measures is tantamount to misassessment when it pertains to bilingual or multicultural clients. There is a growing body of theoretical and empirical support for a bio-ecological approach to assessment (Armour-Thomas & Gopaul-McNicol, in press -a; Ceci, 1990; Sternberg, 1986). There is the notion of a dynamically interactive relationship between cognitive processes and cultural experiences nested within contexts that cannot be understood apart from each other. It would appear that although cognitive processes are biologically programmed, how they are developed and expressed depends on the nature and quality of the cultural experiences within the contexts to which individuals are socialized. In accounting for intellectual behavior the exact contributions of biology and culture remain unclear. This line of thinking has led the above to the conception of intellectual behavior as an inextricable bio-ecological phenomenon and a model of intellectual assessment consistent with this behavior. Chapter 3 examines this bio-ecological approach in great detail. In summary, quantitative and qualitative information culled from both forms of assessment would enable a more comprehensive and nondiscriminatory analysis of the intellectual functioning of people from culturally and linguistically diverse backgrounds (Armour-Thomas & Gopaul-McNicol, in press, -b).

Cross-Cultural Counseling Competencies

With respect to cross-cultural training, researchers (McRae & Johnson, 1991; Ponterotto & Casas, 1987; Sue & Zane, 1987) have addressed the need to develop multicultural competencies in awareness, knowledge, expertise, and boundaries of their competence. Psychologists need to be aware of the values, customs, behavioral patterns, and religious/indigenous beliefs and expectancies of families from divergent cultural/linguistic/ethnic backgrounds. Not only is knowledge about intergroup differences necessary, but intragroup differences as well. This is critical because within certain groups, such as the Hispanic, Asian, and so on, there is much diversity. Different familial role structures, different socialization patterns, and different attitudes must be understood to avoid misassessment of a child. Pedersen (1973) developed the triad training method, which is a videotaped cross-cultural counseling role-play that involves three individuals. One person plays the counselor, a second person plays the client, and a third person plays the pro-counselor (a person from the culture of the client who is a supportive ally to the counselor) or an anti-counselor (an antagonistic force from the client's background who promotes understanding of the potential racial/ethnic conflicts between the counselor and the client). Both the pro- and the anti-counselors' roles are important for training. The former aided in the acquisition of knowledge and skills, and the latter was found to be helpful in developing sensitivity and awareness of personal and cultural biases based on different cultural values. Johnson (1982, 1987, 1990) developed a multicultural training program that included the awareness, knowledge, and skill components. This program focuses on experiential exercises that allow trainees to practice and apply their knowledge gained.

Cross-Cultural Issues in Conflict Resolution

The Worldview Congruence Model (Myers, 1991) discusses how interpersonal conflicts are often a result of eight worldview dimensions: psychobehavioral modality, axiology, ontology, ethos, epistemology, logic, concept of time, and concept of self. Brown and Landrum-Brown (1995) illustrated how worldview conflicts affect the client/counselor/supervisor triadic relationship. These conflicts may result in mistrust and resistance. Thus knowledge of one's view and that of the other party in the relationship would prove beneficial in the therapeutic and supervisory relationship. It is necessary for the supervisor to help the counselor and for the counselor to help the client to identify the ways in which these conflicts affect therapy.

Competence in Special Education Prevention

During the 1995/1996 school year, as I conducted several trainings throughout the state of New York, I was astounded by the sentiments expressed by many practicing psychologists and their supervisors. They repeatedly stated that even if children are not truly handicapped, they have to place them in special education in order to secure some of the services that these children need. Therefore, they diagnose these "borderline" children as learning disabled when in fact they do not have profiles of the typical learning disabled child. An even more disturbing issue which arose is the sentiment that if special education no longer exists, special education teachers will become unemployed. As a result, the institution of special education is necessary, not only for the children, but for the teachers themselves. There seems to be a maintenance of this system whether it is needed or not. Of course, the fact that children in special education do not receive a high school diploma, thus hindering their chances to go on to college, does not seem to be a major concern for these professionals. To say the least, this is quite unethical and unprofessional. At this juncture, what is needed is a transitory placement for these borderline children and training for special education teachers to see themselves more as preventive workers than treatment workers. Psychologists can play a significant role in this enterprise. They can serve as consultants to school personnel in assisting special education teachers to utilize their time in working with regular education "at risk" students to prevent their placement into special education. Thus a mere paradigm shift can ensure the continued employment of special education teachers in another capacity (special education prevention specialists) and, simultaneously, avoid the massive misplacement of children in special education. Training ought to focus on the role of psychologists in expanding the role of special education teachers to the regular education setting.

Competence in Knowing the Bilingual Education Curriculum

Knowing what constitutes a bilingual instructional program for bilingual or limited English proficient children is essential in working with linguistically and culturally diverse children. There is still considerable debate as to whether an ESL or an English immersion program is best suited to meet the needs of bilingual children (Homel et al., 1987). Since this debate is expected to continue for years, psychologists ought to be knowledgeable of the available programs and aware that some children may benefit from a certain type of program and others may benefit from another. In other words, just as there is no single program for monolingual students, no single program can fit all bilingual children. It is critical that this be understood by psychologists who serve as consultants to school personnel.

Competence in Empowering Families through Community-Based Organizations

Competent psychologists have to be able to direct their families to the community-based organizations that can support the school by utilizing their resources in working with handicapped children. After-school tutorial programs, day care centers, free lunch programs, and free clinic care are some examples of community supports that can be used to supply the needed services which the schools are unable to provide. Utilizing the churches, social service agencies, and other outside systems is a way of empowering the families. For example, there are after-school transportation services that can transfer children to and from therapy sessions. Tapping these community resources "is sometimes the single most important interaction in facilitating the possibility of treatment" (Boyd-Franklin, 1989, p. 156).

In addition, if certain necessary services are not available in a particular community, assisting families in forming extended family support networks should be part of the responsibility of the school psychologists.

Competence in Pediatric/Health Psychology

Given the increase in the reported cases of asthma and lead poisoning in the New York City schools, in particular in some of the Bronx and Brooklyn school districts (Brody, 1996), it is critical that psychologists begin to explore the impact of these factors on a child's ability to learn and pay attention. Brody (1996) presents the findings of Dr. Herbert Needleman of the University of Pittsburgh, who found that high levels of lead in the bones of an individual are most likely to lead to aggression, attention difficulties, intellectual deficits, and other social problems.

The New York State Department of Education has already established a "Healthy School Project" in several suburban school districts. Con Edison has been part of this initiative by linking its health awareness program to this Healthy School Project. All of these efforts are aimed at assisting families in detecting, early in their child's education, any medical problems that may impede their child's ability to learn or function effectively in the school system. This is essential in the accurate assessment of a child's handicapping condition. Ruling out any medical problems is one way of preventing misdiagnosis and misplacement.

Competence in Parent Training

Mental health workers can play a major role in educating immigrant parents about the educational and social differences in the U.S. systems (Gopaul-McNicol, Thomas, & Irish, 1991). They can encourage them to attend PTA meetings, explain the issues of confidentiality regarding school records, help them establish contact with community resources, and, all in all, assist in the acculturation process.

All mental health workers can teach parents alternatives to corporal punishment. In summary, helping parents to understand the social and emotional adjustment difficulties their children are experiencing is of major importance in parent training.

Mental health workers also need to alert parents to the reality of special education and the need for them to question the motives of the teacher. Generally speaking, immigrant parents trust their children's teachers and allow placement in special education if the teacher recommends it. They need to be taught about the special education system, since this is a rather foreign concept to most of them. Thomas and Gopaul-McNicol (1991) discuss this in detail. In general, assisting in the acculturation process involves nine important points:

1. Education about the differences in the educational and social systems, with emphasis on alternative disciplinary strategies, the meaning of educational neglect, and the importance of attending parent teacher meetings.

2. Family empowerment, with emphasis on their legal rights.

3. Understanding the family role changes and their effect on acculturation (see Chapter 8).

4. Improving communication between parents and children.

5. Teaching parents how to build or maintain self-esteem in their children.

6. Coping with racism.

7. Teaching parents what support their children need at home and the importance of prioritizing their time.

8. Teaching parents how to cope with rejection from their children due to the children being embarrassed by their parents' accent.

9. Teaching immigrants how to endorse the concept of biculturalism, so that they would not have to live between two worlds.

The question most often asked by parents is: "How can I really raise children without disciplining them? I only know the way I was raised at home." The answer involves not only teaching parents the principles of assertive discipline but in addition helping parents to recognize that since their children are the first generation of Americans, many of their traditional cultural values will be passed on to them. Expediting the process of "Americanization" in a radical way may leave the parents feeling stripped of cultural pride. While it is necessary for parents to understand there are laws that govern them with respect to "child abuse," they must also understand that acculturation for first-generation immigrants is a different process from acculturation for second- and third-generation immigrants. Although some of the traditional values will be passed on, inevitably their children will not have the tremendous allegiance to their native countries as the parents do. Parents must understand that the strong cultural identity may dissipate over time, as each new generation becomes more Americanized. However, immigrant parents ought not to be expected to abandon all of their values, because this can create much anxiety and despair, leaving them very vulnerable and immobilized in a sometimes hostile environment. Instead, these parents need to be taught that the essence and beauty of their culture are some of their traditional values and that to some extent, some of these values can be quite beneficial in helping children to cope. What immigrant families need to be taught is how to take the best from both cultures as they attempt to assimilate in their new country.

CROSS-CULTURAL COMPETENCIES AT THE UNIVERSITY LEVEL

In addition to those competencies listed above, faculty members in psychology programs need to acquire competencies in the areas listed below—consultation and supervision, research, and teaching.

Cross-Cultural Consultation and Supervision

Cross-cultural factors can affect consultation and supervision, such as interracial therapist/client differences, language or dialectical (verbal/nonverbal) differences, social and/or occupational/economic status differences, and differences due to cultural isolation (Brown & Landrum-Brown, 1995). Lefley (1986) emphasized that ongoing evaluation of a counselor's multicultural development needs to be a focus in cross-cultural training. Likewise, educational differences among the client, the counselor, and the supervisor and differences in migration status and geographic origin can affect the perspectives of supervision. This is because any of the above differences can affect the supervisory relationship with respect to content, process, and outcome. Relatedly, these differences can result in resistance to corrective feedback because of the cultural misunderstandings. This can affect the supervisory relationship to the extent that some supervisees systematically refuse to respond to the suggestions of their supervisors in order to maintain the cultural relevance of their therapeutic approaches.

Brown and Landrum-Brown (1995) outlined and critiqued several supervision theories that consider the relevant cross-cultural dimensions that are likely to influence the supervisory process. What is still desperately needed is an expansion of these supervisory models to embody the intercultural dynamic interaction.

Family consultation is in dire need of being addressed since the concept of family has changed immensely over the past fifteen years. Thus the nuclear family with two parents and two children no longer exists. Many cultures emphasize the extended family as a strong financial and emotional support system (Halsell Miranda, 1993). In general psychologists should be able to assist both teachers and parents in planning, implementing, and following up on the child's individual educational program.

Cross-Cultural Research

In addition to the ethical guidelines suggested for all mental health workers, the American Psychological Association (1993), Pedersen (1995), Ponterotto and Casas (1991), Tapp et al. (1974), and Wrenn (1985) outlined some ethical considerations in conducting cross-cultural research:

1. It is necessary to understand the prevailing psychosocial problems, identify the psychocultural strengths in each culture, and examine the community involvement in each culture.

2. It is important to avoid the dangers in defining reality according to particular cultural assumptions. In other words, it is important to understand the client's/culture's worldview.

3. It is important to check with colleagues in and out of the culture to help make good ethical judgments.

4. It is critical to attend to the technical problems of equivalent measurement across cultures. Failure to do so may result in inaccurate interpretations and potentially damaging consequences to the culture being studied.

5. Avoid overuse of a particular culture or a particular population.

6. It is worthy to note that the definition of "privacy" varies culturally. Therefore what may be routine to a Westerner may be highly intrusive to the host culture. As such behaviors that are public to a culture may not be intended for open and public discussion by noncommunity members.

7. The research should be beneficial not only to the researcher, but to the host community as well. The population studied should be enhanced by the research.

Cross-Cultural Teaching—A Proposed Multicultural Curriculum

Bernal and Padilla (1982) called for a multicultural training philosophy. The competencies described above should be infused into the existing psychology program, with each student receiving a one-year internship in a multiethnic/multicultural/multilinguistic school district. In addition, the curriculum should take on a more interdisciplinary approach, utilizing the contributions from related fields such as social work, psychiatry, and anthropology. Exposure to cross-cultural issues in clinical, counseling, social, developmental, and educational psychology can be quite beneficial in cross-cultural training. Moreover, focusing on areas such as psycholinguistics, bilingual/multicultural education, cross-cultural theory, and cross-cultural counseling are all necessary requisites in developing cross-cultural competence. Ethical/legal issues in multicultural assessment, treatment, consultation, supervision, research and so forth, should be infused in each course, not offered only as a separate course. Ridley (1985) suggested that every effort should be made to ferret out the principles that are universal in nature, so that a basis for determining where cultural variability begins and cultural generalization ends would be established. Exposure to various cultural groups should afford students the opportunity to be part of a viable programmatic experience.

Rogers et al. (1992) found that 60 percent of the doctoral and nondoctoral programs they surveyed offered at least one course specifically devoted to multicultural issues and 63 percent of those programs surveyed offered two to five courses. Seventy-five percent of the programs made at least one multicultural course a requirement. Rogers et al. (1992) also found that 27 percent of the programs they surveyed spent less than 5 percent of their time on courses related to minority issues. Forty percent did not spend any time at all on courses addressing a multicultural content, and most of the programs (94 percent) did not require exposure to a foreign language course. As such, the need to develop a specific multicultural curriculum is crucial.

Implementation of the Curriculum

To accomplish this innovative multicultural training program, a step-by-step guideline is outlined below.

1. A written academic policy emphasizing a clear statement of purpose and commitment to cultural diversity, as well as the consequences to the program if these policies are violated. Included in this statement must be definite, quantifiable, tangible program objectives that must be achieved in a particular time frame.

2. Inclusion of cultural and ethnic content should be infused in each course, not taught as a single course only. Thus psychological assessment should be first taught whereby students are exposed to adherence to standardized procedures, and then they should be taught how to step away from standardized testing. Likewise, treatment should allow for cultural consideration throughout the therapeutic courses.

3. There should be more aggressive recruitment of faculty members and students of various cultural backgrounds. Working with an ethnically diverse student and faculty body adds enrichment to the program since one can view issues from various perspectives.

4. Faculty members should be encouraged to update their cross-cultural expertise by attending continuing education courses, seminars, and so on.

The university should give a reduction in their teaching load for one year to allow for this cross-cultural training.

5. A consultant or a full-time faculty member with cross-cultural expertise should be available to consult with all faculty members to assist them in redesigning their curriculum to reflect a diverse cultural content.

6. Funds should be set aside for a few research students to be assigned strictly for this cross-cultural thrust: building a cross-cultural resource file, assisting in student and faculty recruitment, linking with community people to recruit more ethnic minority practicum supervisors, coordinating experts of different cultural backgrounds to speak at colloquia, and so on.

7. Both a faculty member and several students should be allotted to represent ethnic students' concerns.

8. Forming linkages with other departments within the university structure to identify existing cross-cultural courses and experts in cross-cultural studies.

9. Faculty members should be encouraged to attend international conferences not only in European countries, but in "third world" countries as well.

10. For the first two years, an ongoing review of the program to ensure that the goals are being met should be done on a monthly basis at regular staff meetings. After two years of smooth functioning, it should be done on a quarterly basis, and after five years, an annual basis should suffice. Every faculty member should be required to sit in on these meetings.

11. Without all of the above in place and without financial support to fund all of these innovative efforts, failure is most likely to occur. Since the ultimate goal of innovation should be institutionalization, then hard-line financial endowments are needed (Ridley, 1985).

Johnson (1982, 1987, 1990) developed a two-part course that included theory, current research, and a laboratory experiential section. Practica in all areas of the training should be available to ensure that all students receive hands-on training in working with culturally or linguistically different children. Rogers et al. (1992) found that 69 percent of program directors estimated that students were exposed to minority clients less than a quarter of their time during their practicum and internship experiences. Of even greater concern was the finding that almost one-third of the programs surveyed reported that students spent 0–5 percent of their experiential training time with minority clients. This suggests that a large percentage of "school psychology students have limited or no direct exposure to culturally diverse clients during field training" (p. 607). Mio (1989) in his multicultural counseling course allowed students to interact with a person from a different culture on a regular basis over the course of the semester. It was found that these students who were matched with an immigrant student were rated as more culturally sensitive at the end of the semester. Clearly the experiential component helps promote cultural awareness and knowledge of another culture.

A multicultural curriculum should be multifaceted, consisting of a combination of assessment, review of the ethnic literature, personal involvement, and the development of a small classroom group project (Parker et al., 1986). This approach utilizes the cognitive, affective, and behavioral domains. The students should first be assessed on their knowledge, attitudes, and perceptions of cross-cultural experiences, as well as their comfort level in interacting with others from different ethnic and racial groups. This assessment process serves as a guide to the professor for future training. Part two of the course involves readings and discussions about the racial/ethnic literature. Part three is very action oriented in that it involves behavioral activities geared to helping students increase cultural knowledge, sensitivity, and effectiveness. Students initially observe from a distance videotapes and so on and gradually move to participate directly. In the final stage, the students are expected to work on a small-group activity in class. Such a project allows the students to become aware of their own stereotypical values about other racial and ethnic groups.

Multicultural training should also focus on the influence of race in racial identity development (Carter, 1995). Recommendations should be made for White professors who teach multicultural students and cross-cultural issues, as well as minority professors who teach cross-cultural issues to a White student population.

In conclusion, in order to prevent the marginalization of the psychology profession, there is a dire need to make some serious changes to address the growing change in the demographics, in particular in the metropolitan areas. A true commitment to multicultural training requires at minimum the implementation of all of the above. If a multicultural program has only the bare skeleton of a commitment, that creates no more than false generosity (Freire, 1970), dishonesty, and continued disrespect. The goal should be to produce competent psychologists capable of working with children from any linguistic, cultural, or ethnic background.

12
Implications for Future Research and Clinical Work: A Vision for the Mental Health Field

At present, in the school and clinical systems, there are many disciplines which function as multidisciplinary teams. My concern is that each discipline works almost as a separate unit and comes together primarily at meetings of committees on special education mainly to decide on placement for the child.

My hope is that the various disciplines can begin to see the need to be more interdisciplinary than multidisciplinary (see Figure 12.1).

My vision is that administrators can serve as leaders in the school and community systems to bring these various disciplines together with the hope of enhancing the quality of education, and in particular, to bring about a reduction in special education placement.

Thus, with a more interdisciplinary training, administrators can link with guidance counselors and health workers so that school officials will understand which factors are impeding or enhancing the child's functioning.

Likewise, they can work with school psychologists to see how their assessment findings can be used in a prescriptive manner to assist the teachers in the classroom. At this juncture, special education teachers will intervene as special education prevention specialists. Therefore, with the help of these three subdisciplines, children will learn to use all of their strengths to work on their weaknesses. This should result in a reduction of special education placement.

Moreover, administrators can liaison with the social workers and community resource people to develop a pool of resources outside of the school settings to best empower the child and his or her family. If the family is involved in any sort of treatment by psychotherapists, clinical psychologists, psychiatrists, and so on, the administrators can serve as a liaison and can aid school personnel in understanding how the treatment program is enhancing or impeding the child's progress.

Finally, guidance counselors can serve in a consulting capacity, as mediators between the school and vocational organizations outside of the school setting. This is to ensure that there is a connection between completion of high school and job or advanced educational opportunities.

For the mental health field to survive with respect, a multimodal, multisystems approach is needed to address the needs of people from diverse cultural backgrounds.

Figure 12.1
A Multisystem Interdisciplinary Model

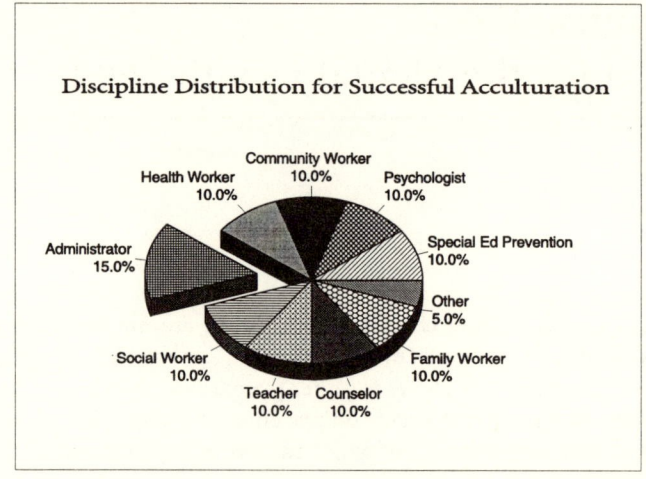

Discipline Distribution for Successful Acculturation

Bibliography

Allen, B. A., & Boykin, A. W. (1992). Children and the educational process: Alienating cultural discontinuity through prescriptive pedagogy. *School Psychology Review, 21*(4), 586–596.

Ambursley, F., & Cohen, R. (1983). *Crises in the Caribbean.* New York: Monthly Review Press.

American Psychiatric Association. (1987). *Diagnostic and statistical manual of mental disorders* (3rd ed. revised). Washington, DC: Author.

American Psychological Association. (1981). Ethical principles of psychologists. *American Psychologist, 36,* 633–681.

American Psychological Association. (1993). Guidelines for providers of psychological services to ethnic, linguistic and culturally diverse populations. *American Psychologist, 48,* 45–48.

Anderson, W., & Grant, R. (1987). *The new newcomers.* Toronto: Canadian Scholars Press.

Aponte, H. (1976). The family-school interview: An ecostructural approach. *Family Process, 15*(3), 303–311.

Aponte, H. & Van Deusen, J. (1981). Structural family therapy. In A. Gurman & D. Kniskern (Eds.), *Handbook of family therapy* (pp. 27–37). New York: Brunner/Mazer.

Armour-Thomas, E. (1992). Intellectual assessment of children from culturally diverse backgrounds. *School Psychology Review, 21*(4), 552–565.

Armour-Thomas, E. (in press). Assessment in the service of thinking and learning for low achieving students. *High School Journal.*

Armour-Thomas, E., & Gopaul-McNicol, S. (in press, -a). A bio-ecological approach to intellectual assessment. In *Cultural diversity and mental health, Vol. 2.*

Armour-Thomas, E., & Gopaul-McNicol, S. (in press, -b). *Assessing intelligence: A bio-ecological model.* Thousand Oaks, CA: Sage Publications.

Arredondo, P., Toporek, R., Pack Brown, S., Jones, J., Locke, D., Sanchez, J., & Stadler, H. (1996). Operationalization of the multicultural counseling competencies. *Journal of Multicultural Counseling and Development, 24*(1), 42–78.

Arredondo-Down, P. (1981). Personal loss and grief as a result of migration. *The Personnel and Guidance Journal, 58,* 376–378.

Asby, D. (1975). Empathy: Let's get the hell on with it. *The Counseling Psychologist, 5*(2), 10–15.

Auerswald, E. (1968). Interdisciplinary versus ecological approach. *Family Process, 7*, 204.

Bache, R. M. (1985). Reaction time with reference to race. *Psychological Review, 11*, 474–486.

Backler, A., & Eakin, S. (1993). *Every child can succeed: Readings for school improvement.* Bloomington, IN: Agency for Instructional Technology.

Bandura, A. (1969). *Principles of behavior modification.* New York: Holt.

Baratz, S., & Baratz, J. (1970). Early childhood intervention: The social science base of institutional racism. *Harvard Educational Review, 40*, 29–50.

Baron, J. (1981). Reflective thinking as a goal of education. *Intelligence, 5*, 291–309.

Baron, J. (1982). Personality and intelligence. In R. J. Sternberg (Ed.), *Handbook of human intelligence* (pp. 109–111). New York: Cambridge University Press.

Barona, A., & Santos de Barona, M. (1987). A model for assessment of limited English proficient students referred for special education services. In S. H. Fradd and W. J. Tikunoff (Eds.), *Bilingual education and bilingual special education: A guide for administrators* (pp. 183–208). San Diego, CA: College Hill Press.

Barona, A., Santos de Barona, M., Flores, A. A., & Gutierrez, M. H. (1990). Critical issues in training school psychologists to serve minority school children. In A. Barona & E. Garcia (Eds.), *Children at risk: Poverty, minority status and other issues in educational equity* (pp. 187–200). Washington, DC: National Association of School Psychologists.

Beckles, H. (1989). *White servitude and black slavery in Barbados.* Knoxville: University of Tennessee Press.

Benedict, F. (1959). *Race: Science and politics.* New York: Viking.

Bereton, B. (1985). *Social life in the Caribbean: 1838–1938.* London: Heisman Kingston.

Bernal, M. (1991, October). Jamaica today. *American Visions* [Special issue], 2–6.

Bernal, M. E., & Padilla, A. M. (1982). Status of minority curricula and training in clinical psychology. *American Psychologist, 37*, 780–787.

Berry, J. (1980). Cultural universality of any theory of human intelligence remains an open question. *Behavioral and Brain Sciences, 3*, 584–585.

Berry, J. W., Kim, U., Minde, T., & Mok, D. (1987). Comparative studies of acculturative stress. *International Migration Review, 21*(3), 491–511.

Berzonsky, M. (1971). The role of familiarity in children's explanations of physical causality. *Child Development, 42*, 705–715.

Binet, A., & Simon, T. (1905). Methods nouvelles pour le diagnostic du niveau intellectual des anormaux. *L'Annee psychologique, 11*, 245–336.

Black, F. W. (1973). Reversal and rotation errors by normal and retarded readers. *Perceptual Motor Skills, 36*, 895–898.

Bogen, E. (1990). *Caribbean immigrants in New York City.* New York: New York City Planning Division, Office of Immigrant Affairs.

Borely, C., & Simmons, H. (1987). *English for CXC.* Surrey, England: Nelson Caribbean.

Borowski, J. G., & Maxwell, S. E. (1985). Looking for Mr. Good-g: General intelligence and processing speed. *Behavioral and Brain Science, 8*(2), 221–222.

Bowen, M. (1978). *Family therapy in clinical practice.* New York: Jason Aronson.

Boyd-Franklin, N. (1989). *Black families in therapy.* New York: Guilford Press.

Boykin, A. W. (1983). The academic performance of Afro-American children. In J. T. Spence (Ed.), *Achievement and achievement motives* (pp. 322–371). San Francisco: Freeman.

Bracken, B. A. (1986). Incidence of basic concepts in the directions of five commonly used American tests of intelligence. *School Psychology International, 7*, 1–10.

Bracken, B. A., & Barona, A. (1991). State of the art procedures for translating, validating and using psychoeducational tests in cross-cultural assessment. *School Psychology International, 12,* 119–132.

Braden, J. P. (1995). For whom the bell tolls: Why the bell curve is important for school psychologists. *School Psychology Review, 24*(1), 27–35.

Bradley, R., Caldwell, B., & Rock, S. (1988). Home environment and school performance: A ten year follow-up and examination of three models of environmental action. *Child Development, 59,* 85.

Bradley, R. H., Caldwell, B. M., Rock, S. L., Ramey, C. T., Barnard, K. E., Gray, C., Gottfried, A. W., Mitchell, S., Hammond, M., Siegel, L. S., & Johnson, D. (1988). Home environment and cognitive development in the first three years of life: A collaborative study involving six sites and three ethnic groups in North America. *Developmental Psychology, 25,* 217–235.

Brand, C. R., & Deary, I. J. (1982). *Intelligence and "inspection time": A model for intelligence.* Berlin: Springer Verlag.

Brannigan, G. G., & Brunner, N. A. (1989). *The modified version of the Bender Gestalt test for preschool and primary school children.* Brandon, VT: Clinical Psychology Publ.

Brannigan, G. G., & Brunner, N. A. (1992). Comparison of the qualitative and developmental scoring systems for the modified version of the Bender Gestalt test. *Journal of School Psychology, 31,* 327–330.

Brice, J. (1982). West Indian families. In M. McGoldrick, J. K. Pearce, & J. Giordana (Eds.), *Ethnicity and family therapy* (pp. 123–133). New York: Guilford Press.

Brice-Baker, J. (1994). Jamaican women. In Comas-Diaz, L. & Greene, B. (Eds.). *Women of color* (pp. 139–160). New York: Guilford Press.

Brislin, R. W. (1970). Back translation for cross-cultural research. *Journal of Cross Cultural Psychology, 1,* 185–216.

Brislin, R. W. (1980). Translation and content analysis of oral and written materials. In H. C. Triandis and J. W. Berry (Eds.), *Methodology: Handbook of cross-cultural psychology:* Vol. 2 (pp. 389–444). Boston: Allyn and Bacon.

Brody, J. (1996). Aggressiveness and delinquency in boys is linked to lead in bones. *New York Times,* Health Section K, p. 4.

Bronfenbrenner, V. (1977). Towards an experimental ecology of human development. *American Psychologist, 45,* 513–530.

Brown, M. T., & Landrum-Brown, J. (1995). Counselor supervision: Cross-cultural perspectives. In J. G. Ponterotto, J. M. Casas, L. A. Suzuki, & C. M. Alexander (Eds.), *Handbook of multicultural counseling* (pp. 263–286). Thousand Oaks, CA: Sage Publications.

Bruner, J. S., Olver, R. R., & Greenfield, P. M. (1966). *Studies in cognitive growth.* New York: Wiley.

Burdoff, M. (1987). The validity of learning potential assessment. In C. S. Lidz (Ed.), *Dynamic assessment: An interactional approach to evaluating learning potential* (pp. 27–42). New York: Guilford Press.

Burke, J., & Tompkins, D. (1991, October). Reggae powerful journey. *American Visions* [Special issue], 10–11.

Burnham, M. A., Hough, R. L., Karno, M., Escobar, J. I., & Telles, C. A. (1987). Acculturation and lifetime prevalence of psychiatric disorders among Mexican Americans in Los Angeles. *Journal of Health and Social Behavior, 28,* 89–102.

Butcher, J. N. (1982). Cross-cultural research methods in clinical psychology. In P. C. Kendall & J. N. Butcher (Eds.), *Handbook of research methods in clinical psychology* (pp. 273–308). New York: John Wiley.

Carey, S. (1985). *Conceptual change in childhood.* Cambridge: MIT Press.

Carlson, J. S. (1985). The issue of g: Some relevant questions. *Behavioral and Brain Science, 8*(2), 224–225.

Carney, C. G., & Kahn, K. B. (1984). Building competencies for effective cross-cultural counseling: A developmental view. *The Counseling Psychologist, 12*(1), 111–119.

Carr, T. H., & McDonald, J. L. (1985). Different approach to individual differences. *Behavioral and Brain Science, 8*(2), 225–227.

Carraher, T. N., Carraher, D., & Schliemann, A. D. (1985). Mathematics in the streets and in schools. *British Journal of Development Psychology, 3,* 21–29.

Carroll, J. B. (1993). *Human cognitive abilities.* Cambridge: Cambridge University Press.

Carter, R. (1995). *The influence of race and racial identity in psychotherapy.* New York: John Wiley & Sons.

Casas, J. M., Ponterotto, J. G., & Gutierrez, J. M. (1986). An ethical indictment of counseling research and training: The cross-cultural perspective. *Journal of Counseling and Development, 64,* 347–349.

Cattell, R. B. (1963). Theory of fluid and crystallized intelligence: A critical experiment. *Journal of Educational Psychology, 54,* 1–22.

Cavalli-Sforza, L., Menozzi, P., & Piazza, A. (1994). *The history and geography of human genes.* Princeton, NJ: Princeton University Press.

Ceci, S. (1990). *On intelligence: More or less.* Princeton, NJ: Prentice Hall.

Charles, E. (1991). Effecting a regional plan for progress. *Caribbean Affairs, 4*(2), 25–30.

Chon, M. (1995). The truth about Asian Americans. In R. Jacoby & N. Glauberman (Eds.), *The bell curve debate* (pp. 238–240). New York: Random House.

Christensen, E. (1975). Counseling with Puerto Ricans: Some cultural considerations. *Personnel and Guidance Journal, 53*(5), 349–356.

Christiansen, J., Thornley-Brown, A., & Robinson, J. (1984). *West Indians in Toronto.* Toronto, Canada: Family Service Association of Metropolitan Toronto.

Clark, C. (1971). The significance of soul. *Contemporary Psychology, 16*(1), 11–12.

Clark, C. (1975). The Shockley-Jensen thesis: A contextual appraisal. *The Black Scholar,* July–August, 3–11.

Clarke, D. (1991). *The impact of foreign born inmates on the New York State Department of Correctional Services.* Albany, NY: New York State Department of Education, Division of Program Planning, Research and Education.

Clarke, K. B., & Clarke, M. P. (1947). *Racial identification and preferences in Negro children: Readings in social psychology.* New York: Holt and Company.

Clarke, V., & Bolarinde, O. (1989). *Adjustment of Caribbean immigrants in New York: Social and economic dimension.* New York: Caribbean Research Center.

Coelho, E. (1976). West Indian students in the secondary schools. *Tesl Talk, 7*(4), 37–46.

Coelho, E. (1991). *Caribbean students in Canadian schools.* Toronto, Canada: Pippin Publishing Ltd.

Cohen, R. (1969). Conceptual styles, culture conflict, and non-verbal tests of intelligence. *American Anthropologist, 71*(5), 828–857.

Cohen, Y. A. (1956). Structure and function: Family organization and socialization in a Jamaican community. *American Anthropologist, 58,* 664–680.

Comas-Diaz, L., & Griffith, E. E. (1988) (Eds.). *Clinical guidelines in cross-cultural mental health.* New York: John Wiley & Sons.

Comer, J., Haynes, N., Joyner, E., & Ben-Avie, M. (Eds.). (1996). *Rallying the whole village: The Comer process for reforming education.* New York: Columbia University Press.

Connelly, J. B. (1983). Comparative analysis of two tests of visual-fine motor integration among Indian and non-Indian children. *Perceptual and Motor Skills, 57*, 1079–1082.

Craig, D. (1966). Teaching English to Jamaican Creole speakers: A model of a multi-dialect situation. *Language Learning, 16*(1 & 2), 49–61.

Cronbach, L. J. (1975). Five decades of public controversy over mental testing. *American Psychologist*, January, 1–14.

Cummins, J. (1984). *Bilingualism and special education: Issues in assessment and pedagogy.* San Diego, CA: College Hill Press.

Cummins, J. (1989). A theoretical framework for bilingual special education. *Exceptional Children, 56*(2), 111–119.

Daniel, E. (1952). *West Indian histories* (Vols. 1–3). London: Thomas Nelson & Sons.

Das, J. P. (1985). Interpretations for a class on minority assessment. *Behavioral and Brain Science, 8*(2), 228–229.

Day, J. D. (1983). The zone of proximal development. In M. Pressley & J. R. Levin (Eds.), *Cognitive strategy research: Psychological foundations* (pp. 155–176). New York: Springer-Verlag.

De Albuquerque, K. (1979). The future of the Rastafarian movement. *Caribbean Review, 8*(4), 22.

De Avila, E. (1974). The testing of minority children: A neo-Piagetian approach. *Today's Education*, November–December, 72–75.

De Avila, E. (1976). Mainstreaming ethnically and linguistically different children: An exercise in paradox or a new approach. In R. L. Jones (Ed.), *Mainstreaming and the minority child* (pp. 65–76). Reston, VA: Council for Exceptional Children.

DeFour, D. (1991). Issues in mentoring ethnic minority students. *Focus, 5*(1), 1–2.

deHirsch, K., Jansky, J., & Langford, S. W. (1986). *Predicting reading failure.* New York: Harper & Row Publishers.

Dillard, J. M. (1983). *Multicultural counseling.* Chicago: Nelson Hall.

Domokos-Cheng Ham, M. A. (1989a). Empathetic understanding: A skill for joining with immigrant families. *Journal of Strategic and Systemic Therapies, 8*(2), 36–40.

Domokos-Cheng Ham, M. A. (1989b). Family therapy with immigrant families: Constructing a bridge between different world views. *Journal of Strategic and Systemic Therapies, 8*, 1–13.

Draguns, J. (1973). Comparisons of psychopathology across cultures. *Journal of Cross Cultural Psychology*, March, 9–47.

Draguns, J. G. (1987). Psychological disorders across cultures. In P. Pedersen (Ed.), *Handbook of cross-cultural counseling and therapy* (pp. 55–62). New York: Praeger.

Dressler, W. (1985). Stress and sorcery in three social groups. *International Journal of Social Psychiatry, 31*(4), 275–281.

Dumas, J. (1989). *Current demographic analysis of Caribbean immigrants in Canada.* Ottawa: Caribbean Government Publishing Center.

Dunn, R. (1978). *Teaching students through their individual learning styles: A practical approach.* Reston, VA: Reston Publishing Co.

Dunn, R., Gemake, J., Jalali, F., & Zenhausern, R. (1990). Cross cultural differences of elementary age students from four ethnic backgrounds. *Journal of Multicultural Counseling and Development, 18*, 23–33.

Edwards, V. K. (1979). *The West Indian student in British schools.* London: Routledge and Kegan Paul.

Edwards, W. F. (1983). Code selection and shifting in Guyana. *Language in Society, 12*(3), 294.

Elliot-Lewis, M. (1989). Responses to problems experienced by immigrant children. In V. Clarke & B. Obede (Eds.), *Adjustment of Caribbean immigrants in New York: Educational dimensions* (pp. 43–56). New York: Caribbean Research Center.

Ellis, A. (1974). *Humanistic psychotherapy: The rational emotive approach.* New York: McGraw Hill Book Co.

Elliston, I. (1985). Counseling West Indian immigrants: Issues and answers. In R. Samuda & A. Wolfgang (Eds.), *Intercultural counseling and assessment: Global perspective* (p. 112). Lewiston, Germany: Hogrefe International Inc.

Eno, L., & Deitchmann, J. (1980). A review of the Bender Gestalt test as a screening instrument for brain damage with school-aged children of normal intelligence since 1970. *The Journal of Special Education, 14,* 37–45.

Erikson, E. (1980). *Identity and the life cycle.* New York: W. W. Norton and Company.

Esquivel, G. (1985). Best practices in the assessment of limited English proficient and bilingual children. In A. Thomas & J. Grimes (Eds.), *Best practices in school psychology I* (pp. 113–123). Washington, DC: National Association of School Psychologists.

Evans-Pritchard, E. E. (1962). *Social anthropology and other essays.* New York: Free Press.

Eysenck, H. J. (1979). *The structure and measurement of intelligence.* Berlin, Germany: Springer.

Eysenck, H. J. (1982). Introduction. In H. J. Eysenck (Ed.), *A model for intelligence* (pp. 1–9). Berlin, Germany: Springer Verlag.

Fabrega, H. (1969). Social psychiatric aspects of acculturation and migration. *Comprehensive Psychiatry, 10*(4), 314–326.

Fairchild, H. H. (1991). Scientific racism: The cloak of objectivity. *Journal of Social Issues, 47*(3), 101–115.

Falicov, C. (1988). Learning to think culturally in family therapy training. In H. Little, D. Breunlin, & D. Schwartz (Eds.), *Handbook of family therapy training and supervision* (pp. 335–357). New York: Guilford.

Feuer, C. H. (1985). The political use of Rasta. *Caribbean Review, 14*(4), 48.

Feuerstein, R. (1979). *The dynamic assessment of retarded performers.* Baltimore: University Park Press.

Fields, S. (1979). Mental health and the melting pot. *Innovations, 6*(2), 2–3.

Figueroa, A. F., Sandoval, J., & Merino, B. (1984). School psychology and limited English proficient children: New competencies. *Journal of School Psychology, 22,* 133–143.

Figueroa, R. A. (1990). Best practices in the assessment of bilingual children. In A. Thomas & J. Grimes (Eds.), *Best practices in school psychology II* (pp. 93–106). Washington, DC: National Association of School Psychologists.

Freire, P. (1970). *Pedagogy of the oppressed.* New York: Seabury Press.

Friedman, E. (1982). The myth of Shiska. In M. McGoldrick, J. K. Pearce, & J. Giordano (Eds.), *Ethnicity and family therapy* (pp. 123–133). New York: Guilford Press.

Frisby, C. L. (1992). Issues and problems in the influence of culture on the psychoeducational needs of African American children. *School Psychology Review, 21*(4), 532–551.

Frisby, C. L. (1995). When facts and orthodoxy collide: The bell curve and the robustness criterion. *School Psychology Review, 24*(1), 12–19.

Fuchs, L. S., & Fuchs, D. S. (1990). Curriculum-based assessment. In C. R. Reynolds and R. W. Kamphaus (Eds.), *Handbook of psychological and educational assessment of children* (pp. 435–455). New York: Guilford Press.

Gardner, H. (1983). *Frames of mind: The theory of multiple intelligences.* New York: Basic Books.

Gardner, H. (1993). *Multiple intelligences.* New York: Basic Books.

Garrett, H. E. (1961). The equalitarian dogma. *Mankind Quarterly, 1,* 253–257.

Ghassemzadeh, H. (1988). A pilot study of the Bender Gestalt test in a sample of Iranian normal children. *Journal of Clinical Psychology, 44*(5), 787–792.

Gibbs, J. T. G., & Huang, L. N. (1989). *Children of color.* San Francisco: Jossey-Bass Publishers.

Gibson, A. (1985). *A light in the dark tunnel.* London: Caribbean House.

Gibson, A. (1986). *The unequal struggle.* London: Caribbean House.

Gickling, E., & Havertape, J. (1981). *Curriculum-based assessment (CBA).* Minneapolis, MN: National School Psychology Inservice Training Network.

Gielen, U. P., Loeb Adler, L., & Milgram, N. A. (1992). *Psychology in international perspective: 50 years of the International Council of Psychologists.* Amsterdam: Swets & Zeilinger.

Giles, R. (1977). *The West Indian experience in British schools.* London: Heinemann London.

Gilgen, A. R., & Gilgen, C. K. (1987). Introduction. In A. R.Gilgen & C. K. Gilgen (Eds.), *International handbook of psychology* (pp. 1–22). New York: Greenwood Press.

Gilmore, G., Chandy, J., & Anderson, T. (1975). The Bender-Gestalt and the Mexican American student: A report. *Psychology in the Schools, 12*(2), 172–175.

Gladstein, G. (1983). Understanding empathy: Integrating counseling, developmental and social psychology perspective. *Journal of Counseling Psychology, 30*(4), 467–482.

Goodstein, C. (1990). America's cities: The new immigrants in the schools. *Crisis, 98*(5), 17–29.

Gopaul-McNicol, S. (1988). Racial identification and racial preference of black preschool children in New York and Trinidad. *Journal of Black Psychology, 14*(2), 65–68.

Gopaul-McNicol, S. (1992a). Understanding and meeting the psychological and educational needs of African American and Spanish speaking students. *School Psychology Review, 21*(4), 529–531.

Gopaul-McNicol, S. (1992b). Implications for school psychologists: Synthesis of the miniseries. *School Psychology Review, 21*(4), 597–600.

Gopaul-McNicol, S. (1993). *Working with West Indian families.* New York: Guilford Press.

Gopaul-McNicol, S., Scully-Demartini, & Diaz (1995). *Examining the visual-motor performance of Latino children with the Koppitz and the Sugar scoring systems.* Paper presented at the Caribbean Research Center Conference. Brooklyn, New York, October.

Gopaul-McNicol, S., Thomas, T. & Irish, G. (1991). *A handbook for immigrants: Some basic educational and social issues in the United States of American.* Brooklyn, NY: Caribbean Diaspora Press.

Gordon, E. W., & Armour-Thomas, E. (1991). Culture and cognitive development. In L. Okagaki & R. J. Sternberg (Eds.), *Directors of development: Influence of the development of children's thinking* (pp. 83–90). Hillsdale, NJ: Lawrence Erlbaum.

Gordon, E. W., & Green, D. (1974). An affluent society's excuses for inequality: Developmental, economic and educational. *American Journal of Orthopsychiatry, 44*(1), 4–18.

Gordon, G. (1980). Bias and alternatives in psychological testing. *Journal of Negro Education, 49*(3), 350–360.

Gordon, R. A., & Rudert, E. E. (1979). Bad news concerning IQ tests. *Sociology of Education, 52,* 174–190.

Gottfried, A. W. (1984). Issues concerning the relationship between home environment and early cognitive development. In A. W. Gottfried (Ed.), *Home environment and early cognitive development* (p. 66). London: Academic Press.

Gould, S. (1981). *The mismeasure of man.* New York: W. W. Norton & Co.

Gushue, G., & Sciarra, D. (1995). Culture and families: A multidimensional approach. In J. Ponterotto, J. Casas, L. Suzuki, & C. Alexander (Eds.), *Handbook of multicultural counseling*. Thousand Oaks, CA: Sage Publications.

Guthrie, R. (1976). *Even the rat was white*. New York: Harper and Row.

Halsell Miranda, A. (1993). Consultation with culturally diverse families. *Journal of Educational and Psychological Consultation, 4*(1), 89–93.

Hargis, C. H. (1987). *Curriculum-based assessment: A primer*. Springfield, IL: Charles C. Thomas.

Hartman, A. (1978). Diagrammatic assessment of family relationships. *Social Casework, 59*, 465–476.

Hartman, A., & Laird, J. (1983). *Family centered social work practice*. New York: The Free Press.

Harwood, A. (1981). *Ethnicity and medical care*. Cambridge, MA: Harvard University Press.

Haynes, N. (1995). How skewed is the bell curve? *Journal of Black Psychology, 21*(3), 275–299.

Helms, J. (1985). Cultural identity in the treatment process. In P. Pedersen, *Handbook of cross-cultural counseling and therapy*. Westport, CT: Greenwood Press.

Helms, J. E. (1989). Eurocentrism strikes in strange places and in unusual ways. *The Counseling Psychologist, 17*, 643–647.

Helms, J. E. (1992). Why is there no study of cultural equivalence in standardized cognitive ability testing? *American Psychologist, 47*(9), 1083–1101.

Hendriques, F. (1953). *Family and color in Jamaica*. London: Eyre and Spottiswoode.

Henry, F. (1982). A note on Caribbean migration to Canada. *Caribbean Review, 11*(1), 38.

Henry, F., & Wilson, P. (1975). Status of women in Caribbean societies: An overview of their social, economic, and sexual roles. *Social and Economic Studies, 24*, 165–198.

Herrnstein, R. J., & Murray, C. (1994). *The bell curve*. New York: The Free Press.

High achieving Asian Americans are fastest growing minority. (1985). *Population Today*, October, pp. 2, 8.

Hilliard, A. G. (1979). Standardization and cultural bias as impediments to the scientific study and validation of "intelligence." *Journal of Research and Development in Education, 12*(2), 47–58.

Hills, H. I., & Strozier, A. L. (1992). Multicultural training in APA approved counseling psychology programs: A survey. *Professional Psychology: Research and Practice, 23*(1), 43–51.

Hinds, D. (1966). *Journey to an illusion*. London: Heinemann.

Holman, A. (1983). *Family assessment: Tools for understanding and intervention*. Beverly Hills, CA: Sage.

Homel, P., Palif, M., & Aaronson, D. (Eds.). (1987). *Childhood bilingualism: Aspects of linguistic, cognitive and social development*. Hillsdale, NJ: Lawrence Erlbaum.

Hoover, M. R., Politzer, L., & Taylor, O. (1991). Bias in reading test for Black language speakers: A sociolinguistic perspective. In A. G. Hilliard (Ed.), *Testing African American students* (pp. 81–98). Morristown, NJ: Aaron Press.

Horn, J. L. (1991). Measurement of intellectual capabilities: A review of theory. In K. S. McGrew, J. W. Werder, & R. W. Woodcock (Eds.), *WJ-R Techincal manual*. Chicago: Riverside.

Hunt, L. (1967). *Immigrants and the youth service*. London: Her Majesty's Stationery Office.

Hutt, M. I. (1977). *The Hutt adaptation of the Bender Gestalt test* (3rd ed.). New York: Grune and Stratton.

Jacobson, E. (1938). *Progressive relaxation*. Chicago: University of Chicago Press.

Jacoby, R., & Glauberman, N. (Eds.). (1995). *The bell curve debate*. New York: Random House.

Jaeger, M. E., & Rosnow, R. L. (1988). Contextualism and its implications for inquiry. *British Journal of Psychology, 79*, 63–75.

James, C. (1990). *Making it.* Oakville: Mosaic Press.

James, C. L. R. (1984). *Party politics in the West Indies.* Port of Spain, Trinidad: Inprint Caribbean Ltd.

James, S. (1978). When your patient is black West Indian. *American Journal of Nursing,* November, 1908–1909.

Jansky, J., & de Hirsch, K. (1972). *Preventing reading failure.* New York: Harper & Row.

Jansky, J. J., Hoffman, M. J., Layton, J., & Sugar, F. (1989). Prediction: A six year follow-up. *Annals of Dyslexia, 39*, 227–246.

Jensen, A. R. (1973). *Educability and group differences.* New York: Harper & Row.

Jensen, A. R. (1974). How biased are culture-loaded tests? *Genetic Psychology Monographs, 90*, 185–244.

Jensen, A. R. (1979). Outmoded theory or unconquered frontier? *Creative Science and Technology, 2*, 16–29.

Jensen, A. R., & Whang, P. A. (1994). Speed of accessing arithmetic facts in long term memory: A comparison of Chinese-American and Anglo-American children. *Contemporary Educational Psychology, 19*, 1–12.

Johnson, S. D. (1982). *The Minnesota, multiethnic counselor education curriculum: The design and evaluation of an intervention for cross-cultural counselor education.* Unpublished doctoral dissertation, University of Minnesota, Minneapolis.

Johnson, S. D. (1987). Knowing that versus knowing how: Towards achieving expertise through multicultural training for counselors. *The Counseling Psychologist, 15*, 320–331.

Johnson, S. D. (1990). Towards clarifying culture, race and ethnicity in the context of multicultural counseling. *Journal of Multicultural Counseling and Development, 18*, 4.

Jones, L. V. (1985). Interpreting Spearman's general factor. *Behavioral and Brain Science, 8*(2), 233.

Justus, J. (1983). West Indians in Los Angeles: Community and identity. In R. Bryce-Laporte (Ed.), *Caribbean immigration into the United States* (pp. 46–58) Washington, DC: Smithsonian Institute.

Karr, S. K. (1982). Bender-Gestalt performance of Sierra Leone, West African children from four sub-cultures. *Perceptual and Motor Skills, 55*, 123–127.

Kashani, J. H., Beck, N. C., Heoper, E. W., Fallhi, C., Corcoran, C. M., McAllister, J. A., Rosenberg, T. K., & Reid, J. C. (1987). Psychiatric disorders in a community sample of adolescents. *American Journal of Psychiatry, 144*, 584–589.

Kerr, M. (1952). *Personality and conflict in Jamaica.* Liverpool, England: Liverpool University Press.

Kim, S. C. (1985). Family therapy for Asian Americans: A strategic-structural framework. *Psychotherapy, 22*, 342–348.

Kiselica, M. S. (1991). Reflections on a multicultural internship experience. *Journal of Counseling and Development, 70*, 126–130.

Koppitz, E. (1981). The Bender Gestalt and vads test performance of learning disabled middle school pupils. *Journal of Learning Disabilities, 14*, 96–98.

Koppitz, E. M. (1975). *The Bender Gestalt test for young children* (Vol. 2). New York: Grune & Stratton.

Korman, M. (1974). National conference on levels and patterns of professional training in psychology: Major themes. *American Psychologist, 29*, 301–313.

Kozol, J. (1991). *Savage inequalities: Children in America's schools.* New York: Crown Publishers, Inc.

Kurtz, B. (1989). Individual differences in cognitive and metacognitive processing. In W. Schneider and F. Weinert (Eds.), *Interactions among aptitudes, strategies and knowledge in cognitive performance.* New York: Springer-Verlag.

Lamur, H., & Speckmann, J. (1975). *Adaptation of the migrants from the Caribbean in the European metropolis.* Paper presented at the 34th annual conference of the American Association of Applied Anthropology, Amsterdam, The Netherlands.

Lane, C. (1995). Tainted sources. In R. Jacoby & N. Glauberman (Eds.), *The bell curve debate* (pp. 125–139). New York: Random House.

Lave, J. (1977). Tailor-made experiments and evaluating the intellectual consequences of apprenticeship training. *The Quarterly Newsletter of the Institute for Comparative Human Development, 1,* 1–3.

Lave, J., Murtaugh, M., & de la Roche, D. (1984). The dialectic of arithmetic in grocery shopping. In B. Rogoff and J. Lave (Eds.), *Everyday cognition: Its development in social context* (pp. 27–39). Cambridge, MA: Harvard University Press.

Lazarus, A. A. (1976). *Multimodal behavior therapy.* New York: Springer.

Leary, P., & De Albuquerque, K. (1989). The other side of paradise: Race and class in the 1986 Virgin Islands elections. *Caribbean Affairs, 2*(1), 51–64.

Lefley, H. P. (1979). Prevalence of potential falling-out cases among Black, Latin and non-White populations of the city of Miami. *Social Science and Medicine, 13B,* 113–128.

Lefley, H. P. (1986). Evaluating the effects of cross-cultural training: Some research results. In H. P. Lefley & P. B. Pedersen (Eds.), *Cross-cultural training for mental health professionals* (pp. 265–307). Springfield, IL: Charles C. Thomas.

Leininger, M. (1969). Witchcraft practices and psychocultural therapy with urban and United States families. *Human Organizations, 32*(1), 73–83.

Lesiak, J. (1984). The Bender visual motor test: Implications for the diagnosis and prediction of reading achievement. *Journal of School Psychology, 22,* 391–405.

Lewis, G. (1983). *In ten years of CARICOM.* Paper presented at a seminar sponsored by the Inter-American Development Bank, Washington, DC.

Lidz, C. S. (1991). *Practitioner's guide to dynamic assessment.* New York: Guilford Press.

London, C. (1978). Sensitizing New York City teachers to the Caribbean student. In H. La Fontaine (Ed.), *Perspectives in bilingual education* (pp. 95–103). Garden City Park, NY: Avery Publishing Group.

London, C. (1980). *Teaching and learning with Caribbean students.* (ERIC Document Reproduction Service No. ED 196 977).

London, C. (1983). Crucibles of Caribbean conditions: Factors for understanding for teaching and learning with Caribbean students in American educational settings. *Journal of Caribbean Studies, 2*(2 & 3), 182–188.

London, C. (1984). Caribbean turning point through education. *The Africana Studies and Research Center Newsletter,* February–March, 1–2.

London, C. (1987). Ethnic composition of New York City schools. In A. Carrasquillo & E. Sandis (Eds.), *Schooling, job opportunities and ethnic mobility among Caribbean youth in the United States* (pp. 27–37). New York: The Equitable.

London, C. (1988). Educational theorizing in an emancipatory context: A case for Caribbean curriculum. *The Journal of Caribbean Studies, 6*(2), 163–178.

London, C. (1989). *Through Caribbean eyes.* Chesapeake, VA: ECA Associates.

London, C. (1990). Educating young new immigrants: How can the United States cope? *International Journal of Adolescence and Youth, 2,* 81–100.

Lonner, W. J. (1981). Psychological tests and intercultural counseling. In P. B. Pedersen, J. G. Draguns, W. J. Lonner, & J. E. Trimbie (Eds.), *Counseling across cultures* (pp. 275–303). Honolulu, HI: East West Center and University of Hawaii.

Lopez, E. C. (1995). Best practices in working with bilingual children. In A. Thomas & J. Grimes (Eds.), *Best practices in school psychology III* (pp. 1111–1121). Washington, DC: National Association of School Psychologists.

Louden, D. (1981). A comparative study of self-concept among minority and majority group adolescents in English multiracial schools. *Ethnic and Racial Studies, 4*(2), 45–46.

Lubin, B., Wallis, R. R., & Paine, C. (1971). Patterns of psychological test usage in the United States: 1935–1969. *Professional Psychology, 2,* 70–74 .

Mabey, C. (1981). Black British literacy. *Education Research, 23*(2), 83–95.

Mabey, C. (1986). Black pupils' achievement in inner city London. *Education Research, 28*(3), 163–173.

Maingot, A., Parry, J. H., & Phillip, S. (1987). *A short history of the West Indies.* London: MacMillan Publishers Ltd.

Marsella, A. J., Kinzie, D., & Gordon, P. (1973). Ethnic variation in the expression of depression. *Journal of Cross-Cultural Psychology, 4,* 435–458.

Marshall, D. (1982). The history of Caribbean migration: The case of the West Indies. *Caribbean Review, 11*(1), 6–11.

Matarazzo, J. (1992). Psychological testing and assessment in the 21st century. *American Psychologist,* August, 1007–1018.

Matthews, J. (1989, March 25). Aspiring lawyers already finding a way to make a point. *The Washington Post,* p. A3.

McGoldrick, M., Pearce, J. K., Giordano, J. (1982). *Ethnicity and family therapy.* New York: Guilford Press.

McGrew, K. S. (1994). *Clinical interpretation of the Woodcock Johnson tests of cognitive ability—revised.* Boston: Allyn and Bacon.

McGrew, K. S. (1995). Analysis of the major intelligence batteries according to a proposed comprehensive Gf-Gc framework of human cognitive and knowledge abilities. In D. P. Flanagan, J. L. Genshaft, & P. L. Harrison (Eds.), *Beyond traditional intellectual assessment: Contemporary and emerging theories, tests and issues.* Manuscript submitted for publication.

McKenzie, M. (1986). Ethnographic findings on West Indian American clients. *Journal of Counseling Psychology Development, 65,* 40–44.

McNerney, M. (1979). The Trinidadian Creole speaker: Performance, awareness and attitude. *Tesl Talk, 10*(1 & 2), 10–18.

McNerney, M. (1980). Teaching English to West Indian students: Developing a comprehensive yet differentiating approach. *Tesl Talk, 11*(1), 26–32.

McNicol, M. (1991). *Helping children adjust to a new culture: A child's perspective.* New York: Multicultural Educational & Psychological Services.

McRae, M. B., & Johnson, S. (1991). Toward training for competence in multicultural counselor education. *Journal of Counseling and Development, 70,* 131–135.

Medway, F. (1995). Best practices in assisting families who move and relocate. In A. Thomas & J. Grimes (Eds.), *Best practices in school psychology III* (pp. 977–985). Washington, DC: National Association of School Psychologists.

Meinchenbaum, D. H. (1977). *Cognitive-behavior modification.* New York: Plenum.

Mercer, J. R. (1973). *Labelling the mentally retarded.* Berkeley: University of California Press.

Mercer, J. R. (1979). In defense of racially and culturally non-discriminatory assessment. *School Psychology Digest, 8*(1), 89–115.

Milkman, R. (1978). A simple exposition of Jensen's error. *Journal of Educational Statistics, 3*(3), 203–208.

Miller, E. L. (1967). *A study of body image, its relationship to self-concept, anxiety and certain social and physical variables in a selected group of Jamaican adolescents.* Unpublished master's thesis, University of the West Indies, Kingston, Jamaica.

Milner, D. (1983). *Children and race.* London: Sage Publications.

Minuchin, S. (1974). *Families and family therapy.* Cambridge, MA: Harvard University Press.

Minuchin, S., Montalvo, B., Guerney, B. G., Jr., Rosman, B. L., & Schumer, F. (1967). *Families of the slums.* New York: Basic Books.

Mio, J. S. (1989). Experiential involvement as an adjunct to teaching cultural sensitivity. *Journal of Multicultural Counseling and Development, 17,* 38–46.

Mitjans-Martinez, A., Cairo-Velarcel, E., Morenza-Padilla, L., Rodriguez-Perez, M. E., & Moros-Fernandez, H. (1987). *La formacion del psicologo en Cuba (English translation): Diseno curricular.* Havana: University of Cuba, Facultad de Psicologia.

Mollica, R. F., Wyshak, G., & Lowelle, J. (1987). The psychosocial impact of war trauma and torture on Southeast Asian refugees. *American Journal of Psychiatry, 144*(12), 1567–1572.

Morrow, R. (1987). Cultural differneces: Be aware. *Academic Therapy, 23*(2), 143–149.

Mosley-Howard, S. (1995). Best practices in considering the role culture. In A. Thomas & J. Grimes (Eds.), *Best practices in school psychology III* (pp. 337–345). Washington, DC: National Association of School Psychologists.

Mowder, B. (1980). A strategy for the assessment of bilingual handicapped children. *Psychology in the Schools, 17*(1), 7–11.

Murtaugh, M. (1985). The practice of arithmetic by American grocery shoppers. *Anthropology and Education Quarterly, 5,* 23–36.

Myers, L. J. (1991). Expanding the psychology of knowledge optimally: The importance of worldview revisited. In R. L. Jones (Ed.), *Black psychology* (3rd ed., pp. 15–28). Berkeley, CA: Cobb & Henry.

Neale, M. D., & McKay, M. F. (1985). Scoring the Bender Gestalt test using the Koppitz developmental system: Interrater reliability, item difficulty, and scoring implications. *Perceptual and Motor Skills, 61,* 627–636 .

New York City Police Department. (1985). Rasta crime. *Caribbean Review, 14*(1), 12.

New York City Police Department, Office of Immigrant Affairs and Population Analysis Division. (1985, May 11). *Caribbean immigrants in New York City: A demographic summary.* Unpublished manuscript presented to the Caribbean Research Center.

Nichols, J., Cheung, P. C., Lauer, J., & Patashnick, M. (1989). Individual differences in academic motivation: Perceived ability, goals, beliefs, and values. *Learning and Individual Differences, 1,* 63–84.

Nichols, R. (1981). Origins, nature and determinants of intellectual development. In M. Begab, H. C. Haywood, & H. Garber (Eds.), *Psychosocial determinants of retarded performance* (Vol. 1) (pp. 11–23). Baltimore: University Park Press.

Noble, C. E. (1969). Race, reality and experimental psychology. *Perspectives in Biology and Medicine, 13,* 10–30.

Oakland, T. (1977). *Psychological and educational assessment of minority children.* New York: Brunner/Mazel.

Oakland, T. (1995). The bell curve: Some implications for the discipline of school psychology and the practices of school psychology. *School Psychology Review, 24*(1), 20–26.

Oakland, T., & Feigenbaum, D. (1979). Multiple sources of test bias on the WISC-r and Bender Gestalt test. *Journal of Consulting and Clinical Psychology, 47*(5), 968–974.

Oakland, T., & Phillips, B. N. (1973). *Assessing minority group children.* New York: Behavioral Publications.

Oberg, P. (1972). Model for culture shock. *The Personnel and Guidance Journal, 2,* 376–378.

Ogbu, J. U. (1978). *Minority education and caste.* Orlando, FL: Academic Press.

Ogbu, J. U. (1988). Black education: A cultural-ecological perspective. In H. P. McAdoo (Ed.), *Black families* (pp. 169–184). Newbury Park, CA: Sage Publishers.

Oldham, J., & Riba, M. (Eds.). (1995). *Review of psychiatry* (Vol. 14). Washington, DC: American Psychiatric Press, Inc.

Padilla, A. M. (1979). Critical factors in the testing of Hispanic Americans: A review and some suggestions for the future. In R. W. Tyler & S. H. White (Eds.), *Testing, teaching and learning: Report of a conference on testing.* Washington, DC: U.S. Government Printing Office.

Palmer, D., Hughes, J., & Juarez, L. (1991). School psychology training and the education of at-risk youth: The Texas A & M University program emphasis on handicapped Hispanic children and youth. *School Psychology Review, 21*(4), pp. 603–616.

Parker, W. M., Valley, M. M., & Geary, C. A. (1986). Acquiring cultural knowledge for counselors in training: A multifaceted approach. *Counselor Education and Supervision, 26,* 61–71.

Parry, J., Sherlock, P., & Maingot, A. (1987). *A short history of the West Indies* (4th ed.). London: MacMillan Publishers Ltd.

Parsons, L., & Weinberg, S. L. (1993). The Sugar scoring system for the Bender Gestalt test: An objective approach that reflects clinical judgment. *Perceptual Motor Skills, 77,* 883–893.

Pasternak, M. (1986). *Helping kids learn multicultural concepts: A handbook of strategies.* Chicago, IL: Research Press Company.

Payne, M. (1989). Use and abuse of corporal punishment: A Caribbean view. *Child Abuse and Neglect, 13,* 389–401.

Pedersen, P. (1973, September). *A cross-cultural coalition training model for educating mental health professionals to function in a multicultural population.* Paper presented at the Ninth International Congress of Ethnological and Anthropological Science, Chicago.

Pedersen, P. (1985). *Handbook of cross cultural counseling and therapy.* Westport, CT: Greenwood Press.

Pedersen, P. (1995). Culture-centered ethical guidelines for counselors. In J. G. Ponterotto, J. M. Casas, L. A. Suzuki, & C. M. Alexander (Eds.), *Handbook of multicultural counseling* (pp. 34–49). Thousand Oaks, CA: Sage Publications.

Philippe, J., & Romain, J. B. (1979). Indisposition in Haiti. *Social Science and Medicine, 13B,* 129–133.

Phillips, A. S. (1976). *Adolescence in Jamaica.* Kingston, Jamaica: Jamaica Publishing House.

Pierre, A. (1986). *New capital arithmetic for the Caribbean.* Kingston, Jamaica: Heinemann Educational Books (Caribbean) Ltd.

Pine, G. J. (1972). Counseling minority groups: A review of the literature. *Counseling and Values, 17,* 35–44.

Plata, M. (1982). *Assessment, placement and programming of bilingual exceptional pupils: A practical approach.* Reston, VA: Council for Exceptional Children.

Plowden, L. (1967). *The Plowden report: Children and their primary schools.* London: Department of Education and Science and Her Majesty's Stationery Office.

Ponterotto, J. G., & Casas, J. M. (1987). In search of multicultural competencies within counselor education. *Journal of Counseling and Development, 64*, 430–434.

Ponterotto, J. G., & Casas, J. M. (1991). *Handbook of racial/ethnic minority counseling research.* Springfield, IL: Charles C. Thomas.

Rabbit, P. M. (1985). Oh g Dr. Jensen! or, g-ing up cognitive psychology. *Behavioral and Brain Science, 8*(2), 238–239.

Ramirez, M., III. (1991). *Psychotherapy and counseling with minorities: A cognitive approach to individual and cultural differences.* New York: Pergamon Press.

Raspberry, W. (1991, May 14). Right strategies for wrong countries. *New York Daily News,* p. 35.

Reid, J. (1986, February). Immigration and the future of U.S. Black population. *Population Today, 14*, 6–8.

Ridley, C. R. (1985). Imperatives for ethnic and cultural relevance in psychology training programs. *Professional psychology: Research and Practice, 16*(5), 611–622.

Rimer, S. (1991, September 16). Between two worlds: Dominicans in New York. *New York Times,* p. B6–L.

Roberts, P. (1988). *West Indians and their language.* London: Cambridge University Press.

Robin, R. W., & Shea, J. D. (1983). The Bender Gestalt visual motor test in Papua New Guinea. *International Journal of Psychology, 18*, 263–270.

Rodriguez-Fernandez, C. M. (1981). *Testing and the Puerto Rican child: A practical guidebook for psychologists and teachers.* Unpublished doctoral dissertation, University of Massachusetts.

Rogers, C. (1975a). What is Rasta? *Caribbean Review, 7*(1), 9.

Rogers, C. (1975b). Empathetic: An unappreciated way of being. *The Counseling Psychologist, 5*(2), 2–10.

Rogers, M., Close Conoley, J., Ponterotto, J., & Wiese, M. J. (1992). Multicultural training in school psychology: A national survey. *School Psychology Review, 21*(4), 603–616.

Rogoff, B. (1978). Spot observations: An introduction and examination. *Quarterly Newsletter of the Institute for Comparative Human Development, 2*, 21–26.

Rogoff, B. (1982). Integrating context and cognitive development. In M. Lamb & A. Brown (Eds.), *Advances in development psychology* (Vol. 2) (pp. 23–40). Hillsdale, NJ: Lawrence Erlbaum.

Rogoff, B., & Chavajay, P. (1995). What's become of research on the cultural basis of intellectual development? *American Psychologist, 50*(10), 859– 877.

Ronstrom, A. (1989). Children in Central America: Victims of war. *Child Welfare League of America, 58*(2), 145–153.

Rosenthal, R., & Jacobson, L. (1968). *Pygmalion in the classroom.* New York: Holt, Rinehart & Winston.

Rosenzweig, M. R. (1992). Psychological science around the world. *American Psychologist, 47*(6), 718–722.

Rothenberg, J. J. (1990). An outcome study of an early intervention for specific learning disabilities. *Journal of Learning Disabilities, 23*(5), 317–320 .

Rothenberg, J. J., Lehman, L. B., & Hackman, J. D. (1979). An individualized learning disabilities program in the regular classroom. *Journal of Learning Disabilities, 12*(7), 72–75.

Rowe, H. (Ed.). (1991). *Intelligence, reconceptualization and measurement.* Hillsdale, NJ: Lawrence Erlbaum.

Rueda, R., Cardoza, D., Mercer, J. R., & Carpenter, L. (1984). *An examination of special education decision making with Hispanics first-time referrals in large urban school districts.* Los Alamitos, CA: Southwest Regional Lab.

Saakana, A. S., & Pearse, A. (1986). *Towards the decolonization of the British educational system.* London: Frontline Journal/Karnak House.

Sabnani, H. B., Ponterotto, J. G., & Borodovsky, L. G. (1991). White racial identity development and cross-cultural counselor training: A stage model. *The Counseling Psychologist, 19*(1), 76–102.

Saeki, C., & Borow, H. (1987). Counseling and psychotherapy: East and West. In P. Pedersen (Ed.), *Handbook of cross-cultural counseling and therapy* (pp. 223–229). New York: Praeger.

Samuda, R. (1975). From ethnocentrism to a multicultural perspective in educational testing. *Journal of Afro-American Issues, 3*(1), 4–17.

Samuda, R. (1976). Problems and issues in assessment of minority group children. In R. L. Jones (Ed.), *Mainstreaming and the minority child* (pp. 65–76). Reston, VA: Council for Exceptional Children.

Sapp, G. L. (1984). *Sociocultural factors and Bender visual-motor Gestalt performance.* Paper presented at the annual convention of the National Association of School Psychologists, Philadelphia, Pennsylvania.

Sattler, J. M. (1988). *Assessment of children.* San Diego, CA: Jerome M. Sattler Publisher.

Sattler, J. M., & Gwynne, J. (1982). Ethnicity and Bender visual motor test performance. *Journal of School Psychology, 20*(1), 69–71.

Schacter, S., Brannigan, G. G., & Tooke, W. (1991). Comparisons of two scoring systems for the modified revision of the Bender Gestalt test. *Journal of School Psychology, 29,* 265–269.

Schaefer, E. S. (1987). Parental modernity and child academic competence: Towards a theory of individual and societal development. *Early Development and Care, 27,* 373–389.

Schmidt, P. (1990, April 18). School reports progress in assessing limited English proficient students. *Education Week, 18,* 1–2.

Scobie, E. (1972). *Black Britannia.* Chicago, IL: Johnson Publishing Company.

Scribner, S. (1986). Thinking in action: Some characteristics of practical thought. In R. Sternberg & R. K. Wagner (Eds.), *Practical intelligence: Nature and origins of competence in the everyday world* (pp. 112–126). New York: Cambridge University Press.

Semaj, L. (1979). Inside Rasta: The future of a religious movement. *Caribbean Review, 14*(1), 8.

Sewell-Coker, B., Hamilton-Collins, J., & Fein, E. (1985). Social work practice with West Indian immigrants. *Social Casework: The Journal of Contemporary Social Work,* November, 563–568.

Shapiro, E. (1990). An integrated model for curriculum based assessment. *School Psychology Review, 19*(3), 331–349.

Shapiro, E. S. (1987). *Behavioral assessment in school psychology.* Hillsdale, NJ: Lawrence Erlbaum.

Shinn, M. R. (Ed.). (1989). *Curriculum-based measurements: Assessing special children.* New York: Guilford Press.

Shon, S. P., & Ja, D. Y. (1982). Asian families. In M. McGoldrick, J. K. Pearce, & J. Giordano (Eds.), *Ethnicity and family therapy* (pp. 123–133). New York: Guilford Press.

Short, G. (1985). Teacher expectation and West Indian underachievement. *Educational Research, 27*(2), 95–101.

Siegel, L. S. (1984). Home environmental influence on cognitive development in preterm and full-term children during the first five years. In A. W. Gottfried (Ed.), *Home environment and early cognitive development* (pp. 62–77). Orlando, FL: Academic Press.

Silvera, M. (1986). *Silenced.* Toronto: Williams Wallace Production, Inc.

Singleton, R. A., Straits, B. C., & Straits, M. M. (1993). *Approaches to social research* (2nd ed.). New York: Oxford University Press.

Skinner, B. F. (1974). *About behaviorism.* New York: Knopf.

Sloan, T. S (1990). Psychology for the third world. *Journal of Social Issues, 46*(3), 1–20.

Snyder, R. T., Holowenzak, S. P., & Hoffman, N. (1971). A cross-cultural item-analysis of Bender Gestalt protocols administered to ghetto and suburban children. *Perceptual and Motor Skills, 33,* 791–796.

Snyderman, M., & Rothman, S. (1987). Survey of expert opinion on intelligence and aptitude testing. *American Psychologist, 42,* 137–144.

Solomon, P. (1992). *Black resistance in high school.* Albany: State University of New York Press.

Soutar-Hynes, M. (1976). West Indian realities in the intermediate grades: The emerging role of the ESD teacher. *Tesl Talk, 7*(4), 31–36.

Sowell, T. (1981). *Ethnic America.* New York: Basic Books.

Sternberg, R. J. (1984). What should intelligence tests test? Implications of a triarchic theory of intelligence for intelligence testing. *Educational Researcher,* January, 5–15.

Sternberg, R. J. (1985). *Beyond IQ.* New York: Cambridge University Press.

Sternberg, R. J. (1986). *Intelligences applied.* New York: Harcourt Brace Jovanovich, Publishers.

Sternberg, R. J., & Powell, J. S. (1983). Comprehending verbal comprehension. *American Psychologist, 38,* 878–893.

Sternberg, R. J., Wagner, R. K., & Okagaki, L. (1993). Practical intelligence: The nature and role of tacit knowledge in work and at school. In H. Reese & J. Puckett (Eds.), *Advances in lifespan development* (pp. 205–227). Hillsdale, NJ: Earlbaum.

Stetson, B. R. (1934). The investigation of racial differences prior to 1910. *Journal of Negro Education, 2,* 39–44.

Stewart, R. (1986). *The United States in the Caribbean.* London: Heinemann Educational Books, Inc.

Sue, D., Arredondo, P., & McDavis, R. (1992). Multicultural counseling competencies and standards: A call to the profession. *Journal of Multicultural Counseling and Development, 20,* 64–88.

Sue, D. W., & Sue, D. (1990). *Counseling the culturally different: Theory and practice* (2nd ed.). New York: John Wiley.

Sue, S. (1981). *Counseling the culturally different.* New York: Wiley.

Sue, S., & Zane, N. (1987, January). The role of culture and cultural techniques in psychotherapy. *American Psychologist, 42,* 37–45.

Sugar, F. (1992). A new method for scoring the Bender Gestalt test of visual motor development. Unpublished manuscript, The Dalton School, New York.

Super, C. M. (1980). Cognitive development: Looking across at growing up. *New directions for child development: Anthropological perspectives on child development, 8,* 59–69.

Suzuki, D. (1995). Correlation as causation. In R. Jacoby & N. Glauberman (Eds.), *The bell curve debate* (pp. 280–282). New York: Random House.

Suzuki, S. (1969). *Nurtured by love.* New York: Exposition Press.

Tapp, J. L., Kelman, H., Triandis, H., Wrightsman, L., & Coelho, G. (1974). Advisory principles for ethical considerations in the conduct of cross-cultural research: Fall 1973 revision. *International Journal of Psychology, 9*, 231–349.

Taylor, R. (1984). *Assessment of exceptional students: Educational and psychological procedures.* Englewood Cliffs, NJ: Prentice-Hall.

Taylor, R. L., Kaufman, D., & Partenio, I. (1984). The Koppitz developmental scoring system for the Bender Gestalt: Is it developmental? *Psychology in the Schools, 21*, 425–428.

Taylor, R. L., & Partenio, I. (1984). Ethnic differences on the Bender Gestalt: Relative effects of measured intelligence. *Journal of Consulting and Clinical Psychology, 52*(5), 784–788.

Thomas, T. (1991, August). *Post traumatic stress disorder in children.* Paper presented at the annual meeting of the American Psychological Association, Boston, MA.

Thomas, T., & Gopaul-McNicol, S. (1991). *An immigrant handbook on special education in the United States of America.* New York: Multicultural Educational & Psychological Services.

Thomas, W. B. (1986). Mental testing and tracking for the social adjustment of an urban underclass, 1920–1930. *Journal of Education, 168*(2), 9–30.

Thrasher, S., & Anderson, G. (1988). The West Indian family: Treatment challenges. *Social Casework: Journal of Contemporary Social Work, 5*, 171–176.

Thurstone, L. L. (1924). *The nature of intelligence.* New York: Harcourt Brace.

Triandis, H. (1987). Some major dimensions of cultural variation in client populations. In P. Pedersen (Ed.), *Handbook of cross-cultural counseling and therapy* (pp. 21–28). New York: Praeger.

Triandis, H., & Brislin, R. (1984). Cross cultural psychology. *American Psychologist, 52*, 1006–1009.

Trinidad plans to fight deportation. (1991, September 16). *Regional Newspaper for the North Eastern Caribbean*, p. 2.

Troike, R. (1968). Social dialects and language learning: Implications for TESOL. *TESOL Quarterly, 2*(3), 176–180.

Tseng, W., Xu, D., Ebata, K., Hsu, J., & Cul, Y. (1986). Diagnostic pattern for neuroses among China, Japan and America. *American Journal of Psychiatry, 143*, 1010–1014.

Tucker, J. A. (1980). *Nineteen steps for assuring non-biased placement of students in special education.* Reston, VA: ERIC Clearinghouse on Handicapped and Gifted Children.

U.S. Department of Commerce. (1989, October 12). Hispanic population surpasses 20 million mark; grows by 39 percent, Census Bureau reports. (Census Bureau Press Release 89–58).

Valencia, R., Henderson, R., & Rankin, R. (1981). Relationship of family constellation and schooling to intellectual performance of Mexican American children. *Journal of Educational Psychology, 73*(4), 524–532.

Valere-Meredith, J. (1983). *Factors involved in the pidginization process of the English negative system.* Unpublished manuscript.

Valere-Meredith, J. (1985). *Problems in the methodology in the teaching of English as a second dialect.* Unpublished manuscript.

Valere-Meredith, J. (1989). *Teaching English as a second dialect for illiterate West Indians in Canada.* Unpublished manuscript.

Vandenberg, S. G. (1965). Multivariate analysis of twin differences. In S. G. Vandenberg (Ed.), *Methods and goals in human behavior genetics* (pp. 71–90). New York: Academic Press.

Vasquez-Nuttall, E., Goldman, P., & Landurand, P. (1983). *A study of mainstreamed limited English proficient handicapped students in bilingual education.* Newton, MA: Vasquez-Nuttall Associates.

Vaughn, B. E., Block, J. E., & Block, J. (1988). Parental agreement on child-rearing during early childhood and the psychological characteristics of adolescents. *Child Development, 59,* 1020–1033.

Vernon, P. E. (1982). *The abilities and achievements of Orientals in North America.* New York: Academic Press.

Vygotsky, L. S. (1978). *Mind in society: The development of higher psychological processes.* Cambridge, MA: Harvard University Press.

Walker, J. (1984). *The West Indians in Canada.* Ottawa, Canada: Keystone Printing and Lithographing Ltd.

Walter, R. (1983). *The groundings with my brothers.* London: Bogle-L'Ouverture Publications Ltd.

Waters, A. M. (1984). *Race, class, and political symbols.* New Brunswick, NJ: Transaction Books.

Wechsler, D. (1958). *The measurement and appraisal of adult intelligence* (4th ed.). Baltimore: Williams & Wilkins.

Weidman, H. (1979). Falling-out: A diagnostic and treatment problem viewed from a transcultural perspective. *Social Science and Medicine, 13B,* 95–112.

Welsing, F. C. (1974). The Cress theory of color confrontation. *The Black Scholar, 6,* 26–38.

Werner, O., & Campbell, D. T. (1970). Translating, working through interpreters and the problem of decentering. In R. Naroll & R. Cohen (Eds.), *A handbook of method in cultural anthropology* (pp. 398–420). New York: The Natural History Press.

Whimbey, A. (1975). *Intelligence can be taught.* New York: Dutton Press.

Whitaker, C. (1986). The West Indian influence. *Ebony, 41*(7), 135–144.

Wilen, D. K., & Sweeting, V. M. C. (1986). Assessment of limited English proficient Hispanic students. *School Psychology Review, 15*(1), 59–75.

Williams, E. (1967). *Capitalism and slavery.* London: Lowe & Brydone Printers Ltd.

Williams, E. (1981). *Forge from the love of liberty.* Port of Spain, Trinidad: Longman Caribbean.

Williams, R. (1971). Abuses and misuses in testing black children. *Washington University Magazine, 41*(3), 34–37.

Williams, R. (1975). The BITCH-100: A culture-specific test. *Journal of Afro-American Issues, 3,* 103–106.

Williams, R. (1980). Scientific racism and IQ: The silent mugging of the black community. *Psychology Today, 7*(12), 32–41.

Wittkower, E. D. (1964). Spirit possession in Haitian voodoo ceremonies. *Acta Psychother, 12,* 72–80.

Wober, M. (1974). Towards an understanding of the Kiganda concept of intelligence. In J. W. Berry & P. R. Dasen (Eds.), *Culture and cognition: Readings in cross-cultural psychology* (pp. 101–115). Germany: Methuen.

Woodcock, R. E. (1990). Theoretical foundations of the WJ-R measures of cognitive ability. *Journal of Psychoeducational Assessment, 8,* 231–258.

Wrenn, C. G. (1985). Afterword: The culturally encapsulated counselor revisited. In P. Pedersen (Ed.), *Handbook of cross-cultural counseling and therapy* (pp. 323–329). Westport, CT: Greenwood Press.

Yee, A. H. (1983). *Ethnicity and race: Psychology perspectives.* London: Karnak House.

Yekwai, D. (1988). *British racism: Miseducation and the Afrikan child.* London: Karnak House.

Young, L., & Bagley, C. (1979). *Identity, self-esteem and evaluation of color and ethnicity in young children in Jamaica and London.* Paper presented at the 3rd annual conference of the Society of Caribbean Studies, London.

Ysseldyke, J. (1990). Goodness of fit of the Woodcock-Johnson psycho-educational battery—Revised to the Horn-Cattell Gf-Gc theory. *Journal of Psychoeducational Assessment, 8,* 268–275.

Ysseldyke, J. E. & Marston, D. (1982). A critical analysis of standardized reading tests. *School Psychology Review, 11,* 257–266.

Index

About the Author

SHARON-ANN GOPAUL-MCNICOL is Associate Professor at Howard University and Executive Director of Multicultural Educational and Psychological Services. She is the author of *Working with West Indian Families* (1993).

ISBN 0-275-95560-5

90000>

EAN

9 780275 955601

HARDCOVER BAR CODE